Colorado:
Crossroads of the West
Matthew T. Downey and Fay D. Metcalf

PRUETT **P** *PUBLISHING COMPANY*
Boulder, Colorado

Library of Congress Cataloging in Publication Data

Downey, Matthew T
   Colorado: crossroads of the West.

   Bibliography: p.
   SUMMARY: A history of Colorado from earliest times
to the present.
   1. Colorado — History — Juvenile literature. (1. Colorado — History) I. Metcalf, Fay D., 1928- joint
author. II. Title.
F776.3.D68 978.8 76-25857
ISBN 0-87108-204-7

Colorado state emblem photographs courtesy Colorado Department
of Public Relations.

*All photographs courtesy of the State Historical Society of
Colorado, excepting line illustrations and photographs
otherwise acknowledged. Every effort has been made to
obtain written permission for photographs appearing in
chapter eleven. Oral permission was granted in all ins-
tances.*

First Edition

    2   3   4   5   6   7   8   9   0

Printed in the United States of America

To Beth, Tom, and Sarah

Preface

This book is a history of Colorado for students in elementary schools. It uses a social and cultural approach. We want to help students understand that people of various cultural traditions have lived in the area we now call Colorado. Many aspects of this cultural diversity still survive today. We have tried to give the students something of an insider's view of these different ways of life.

We wish to thank the many people who have contributed to this book. We especially wish to acknowledge our debt to the elementary teachers from Boulder, Longmont, Loveland, and Westminster who participated in an in-service workshop on Colorado history in the spring of 1974. It was during the workshop that we discovered the need for a book such as this. One of those teachers, Phyllis J. Clarke of Heatherwood Elementary School, Boulder, is largely responsible for the teachers' guide accompanying this text.

Several teachers and historians contributed ideas and helpful criticism during the writing of the book. Four elementary teachers from the Boulder Valley Re 2 school district — Ellen Kasynski, Velda Tanguay, Betty Mason, and Helen Klein — read and criticised several chapters at an early stage in the writing. Errors of fact and interpretation were avoided because of the careful reading of the entire text by Professor Liston Leyendecker of Colorado State University and Professor Robert G. Athearn of the University of Colorado. Euvaldo Valdez, assistant principal of Boulder High School and Professor William D. Taylor of the University of Colorado gave us ideas and valuable criticism for the chapter on the Spanish-Americans. The authors accept full responsibility for any errors that may remain.

We wish to thank the State Historical Society of Colorado for its assistance. Most of the photographs in the book came from the historical society's files. Several of the drawings are based on artifacts in the state historical museum's collections. Unpublished materials in the historical society's library provide several of the biographical vignettes included in the book.

The maps, illustrations, and logos were drawn by Mike Spencer. We greatly appreciate the help of Ruth Major, who did the typing.

We wish to thank the publishers for permission to quote from the following sources: Rifle Reading Club, *Rifle Shots* (Rifle, Colo.: Rifle Reading Club, 1973), Althea Bass, *The Arapaho Way* (New York: Crown Publishers, Inc., 1966), and *Colorado Magazine*, State Historical Society of Colorado (Luis Baca, "The Guadalupita Colony of Trinidad," in volume 21, January 1944, page 24).

Finally, we thank the University of Colorado Centennial Commission for a grant which solved many of the problems involved in preparing the book for publication.

MTD
FDM
February 1976

Contents

Digging into the past
Photograph provided by authors

An archeological site
Photograph provided by authors

1

The Early People

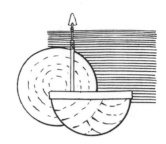

Different kinds of people have lived in the area that we now call Colorado. Indians, people from Mexico, white and black Americans, and many others have called this land their home. They have lived in many different ways. Some of these people have lived in tepees. Others have lived in houses made of wood. They have lived in big cities, on ranches, and in homes built in caves. They have been different in many ways, but they have all had one thing in common.

All of the people have used the land to make a living for themselves and their families. Some made a living on the plains. Others did so in the mountains and in the river valleys. They learned to use the plants and the animals, the water, and the minerals under the ground. But they used these things in many different ways. We shall see how different the use of the land really was.

These people had something else in common. All of them came here from some other place. Some came from Mexico. Others came from the states in the East. Many came from other countries far away. Even the earliest people came to the land that is now Colorado from some other place. That was a long time ago.

When did the first people come to what is now Colorado? No one knows for certain. It was a very, very long time ago. Maybe it was fifteen or twenty thousand years ago. That was long before anyone had learned to read or write. People had not yet learned to make things out of metal. Can you imagine what life here was like that long ago? Finding out about people who lived thousands of years ago is not easy. Nobody is alive who can remember what life was like then. The people left no books or pictures telling about their lives. We have to find out in another way.

How could you find out about other people who live in Colorado today? Which of these would you do first?
Turn on the television.
Read in the newspaper.
Talk to people and ask questions.

Finding out about the very early people who lived here is like a mystery story. We have to look for clues. What did the people leave behind? What facts can we gather? The clues are not easy to find. Often they are buried deep in the ground. They are covered up by dust and dirt blown by the winds over thousands of years. Still, many people have found such clues.

Some clues about early man in Colorado
Photograph by Robert Frazier

Some of the people who look for these clues are called archeologists. They find out about the past by studying the things people have left behind. Pottery, bones, beads, and stone tools all tell a story to the archeologists. Even trash piles are useful to them. Archeologists can learn much from what people throw away. Graves in which people were buried can also tell a story. In the early times, many of the things people used every day were buried with them. Such clues tell us some things about the early people of Colorado.

What could someone find out about you and your family from looking at things in your trash can?

Archeologists at work
Photo provided by authors

Folsom Man

We know about some of the early people from clues that were found near the small town of Folsom, New Mexico. One day about the year 1900, a black cowboy named George McJunkin found some old bones. They were sticking out of the side of a ditch nearly 12 feet down. He got down from his horse to look at them closely. They were bigger than cattle or buffalo bones. He had never seen bones like these before. McJunkin dug up some of the bones and took them home to show his friends.

Many years later an archeologist named J. D. Figgins found out about the bones. He knew that they came from a buffalo that had lived more than ten thousand years ago. These animals were much bigger than buffalo are today. Figgins went to Folsom and found more of these bones. No less than 30 buffalo had died there. When he started digging up the bones he also found some stone points that looked like big arrowheads. Did this mean that the buffalo were killed by people? Did the bones and the points belong together? Or were the stone points left there at a more recent time? In those days, no one thought that people had lived in America that long ago.

Figgins wanted to know if people really had killed these buffalo thousands of years ago. After two summers of careful digging, he made a great find. There in the dirt was a stone point lying between two buffalo rib bones. He was very excited. These were the clues that solved the mystery.

What did the clues tell Figgins?

Figgins saw that the buffalo was killed by a person who had thrown a spear. It proved that people had lived in America a very long time ago. One of the hunters who had killed the buffalo had lost a spear point. It was stuck between the ribs where he could not find it. After that buffalo was killed, thousands of years had passed and the bones were covered deep with dust and dirt. All of the clues about these people were buried deep in the ground until George McJunkin found the old bones.

Archeologists named the spear points after the little town nearby. They are called Folsom Points. The people who killed the buffalo are known as Folsom Men. Later on, Folsom Points were also found in other places. Many have been found in Colorado. We know that Folsom Man was one of the early people living here.

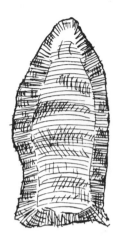

Folsom point

This is what you might have seen had you lived near what is now Folsom, New Mexico, 10,000 years ago. Can you tell a story about this picture? What clues might these hunters have left behind?

What do the clues tell us about Folsom Man? We know that he hunted buffalo, but we know little else. No houses that Folsom Man may have lived in have been found. Perhaps he lived in caves. What did Folsom Man look like? How tall were these people? We do not know. The archeologists have found only where Folsom Man was. They have not yet found Folsom Man himself.

Clovis and Sandia Man

Were Folsom Men the first people to live in what is now Colorado? Probably not. Other bones and stone points found here seem even older. Some of the bones came from a kind of elephant called a mammoth. The mammoth may have disappeared before Folsom Man arrived. Some of the same bones and points were also found near Clovis, New Mexico. Archeologists named the people who made the points Clovis Man. Maybe Clovis Man was not the first people to live here, either. There are still older clues.

One day, some Boy Scouts were hiking in the Sandia Mountains in New Mexico. They found a big cave. On the floor of the cave, there was some broken pottery. An archeologist named Frank Hibben went to look at the cave. He started to dig. First he found more pottery. But it was only a few hundred years old. He dug deeper and found buffalo bones and Folsom points. He kept on digging. Finally he found bones of extinct horses, camels, mammoths, and another kind of elephant — the mastodon. These bones had spear points beside them, too. They were not like any points found before. The makers of these points were named Sandia Man. These people may have lived thousands of years before Folsom Man. Maybe they lived fifteen or twenty thousand years ago. Did Sandia Man hunt in the area that is now Colorado? We do not know.

Clovis point

Sandia point

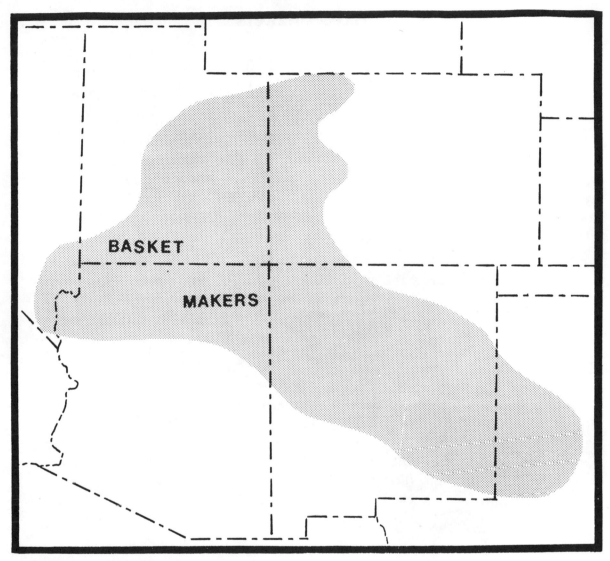

BASKET

MAKERS

Early People of the Southwest
These people lived in an area that later
became four states. Find out the names of
the states.

The Basketmakers

People called the Basketmakers also lived here in the early days. They arrived thousands of years after Folsom Man. Richard Wetherill was the first to find clues about them. He was a cowboy who became an archeologist. We shall meet him again later in this book. In 1893, he and others were digging in a large cave in Utah. There he found some graves of people who lived long ago. Buried with the dead people were food, clothes, spear points, and many baskets. These were things they had used during life.

Do you know why these things were buried with the people?
Why did the Basketmakers think that dead people would need these things?

Richard Wetherill had never seen so many baskets before. They were very well made. Some even had pretty colors woven into them. He found baskets of many shapes and sizes. The people who made them must have had many uses for baskets. Wetherill decided to call these people the Basketmakers.

Can you think how the Basketmakers could have carried water in a basket? Do you know how they might have cooked in a basket? What is this woman doing?

We know more about the Basketmakers than about Folsom Man. They left more clues behind. The bodies of Basketmaker people have also been found. We even know what these people looked like. They were short people. The women were about five feet tall. The men were a little taller. They had brown skin and black hair. In the caves where Basketmaker people lived, archeologists have found holes or pits dug in the ground. Grains of corn were found in some of the pits.

A Basketmaker's cave

This clue tells us that the Basketmakers had learned how to farm. By growing corn, and later on beans and squash, they did not have to depend on only hunting for food.

In the earliest times, the Basketmakers lived out in the open or in caves. While that would not be too bad in the summer, it was hard on them in the winter. So the Basketmakers learned to make houses. They were used to living in caves, and they knew how to dig pits in the caves to store food. This gave them the idea for their first houses, which were pit houses inside caves. Partly above ground and partly below, these houses were made of poles and dried mud. The door was a hole in the flat roof with a ladder sticking out. But why build a house in a cave? Caves are dark and gloomy. Why not build it out in the open?

Pit houses in a cave

Some Basketmaker must have asked himself that question. Later on the houses were built in the open. Whole villages of pit houses were built in the valleys and on the mesas. Later on, the Basketmakers changed the way they built their houses. Some of the rooms were built on top of the ground and each house was joined to the next one. Each village was a row of houses. In front, there were underground rooms like the old pit houses.

As the years passed, the Basketmakers learned many things. They learned to make pottery out of clay.

Later the Basketmakers built villages like this

A clay pot was easier to cook in than a basket. The Basketmakers also learned to use the bow and arrow. It became easier to kill animals when they did go hunting. How did they learn these things? They may have learned them from other tribes. A new idea like the bow and arrow spread quickly from tribe to tribe.

When all this was happening, Folsom Man was no longer around. How surprised he would have been if he could have walked into a Basketmaker village. People farming and living in houses! Clay pots and bows and arrows! Such modern things! He would have learned a lot that day. Above all, he would have learned that the land we call Colorado could be used in different ways. Many different kinds of people could live here.

Looking Backward and Forward

Who were these early people? Where did they come from? What happened to them? We can still only partly answer these questions. We need more clues. It is still a mystery story.

They may have come from Asia thousands of years ago. In the far north, Asia and America are almost joined together. There are only a few miles of water between them. In the winter the water may have frozen over. The first people may have walked across the ice and slowly moved south. Did the people who made the Folsom or Sandia Points come across the ice?

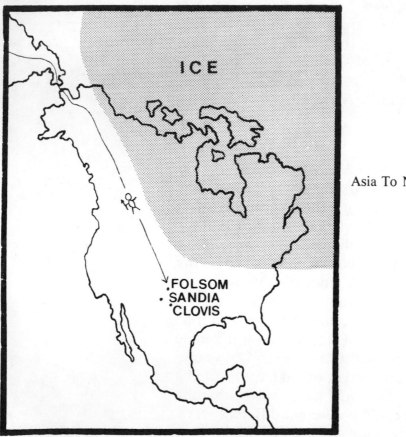

Asia To North America

We do not really know. Maybe their ancestors did thousands of years before.

What happened to these early people? For Folsom Man, we do not have enough clues. Maybe they moved on to hunt some place else. We think we know about the Basketmakers. They remained here as early Indian farmers. Hundreds of years later, people related to them were still living here. They were the Indians of Mesa Verde. They no longer made baskets, and their life had changed in other ways. That part of the story comes next.

Mesa Verde
Photos provided by authors

2

The Cliff Dwellers

It was a snowy Colorado day in December 1888. The cowboys rode slowly into the canyon. Richard Wetherill and Charlie Mason had never been in this canyon before. It was far away from their ranch down on the Mancos River. They were looking for stray cattle. They rode on, following cattle tracks up the canyon. The tracks led up to the top of a high mesa. The Spanish had named it Mesa Verde. That meant the Green Mesa. Mesa was also a Spanish word. It meant table. The Mesa Verde was flat like a table on top and green with juniper trees. Richard and Charlie hoped they would find their cattle up on the mesa.

Few outsiders had explored the Mesa Verde. It was Ute Indian country. But these two cowboys were friends of the Utes. The Utes had often visited their ranch on the Mancos. They told them strange stories about the Mesa Verde. The Utes said there were many caves in the canyon walls. Some of them were filled with rooms. These were the homes of Indians long ago. No one lived there now. The Utes were afraid to go near them. They thought the spirits of the dead were still there.

A Ute named Acowitz told the cowboys about one very big cave. He said that hundreds of Indians had lived in its many rooms. The cowboys could hardly believe Acowitz. A cave that hundreds of people had lived in? They had once seen some small caves with rooms, but a whole city built in a cave? Who could believe that?

The cowboys riding up the canyon remembered Acowitz's story. Soon they were on top of the mesa.

"Charlie, look at that!" Richard shouted.

He sat still on his horse, pointing across a canyon. In the canyon wall was the biggest cave they had ever seen. It was filled from one end to the other with rooms. Some of the stone rooms were four stories high. It was a city in a cave.

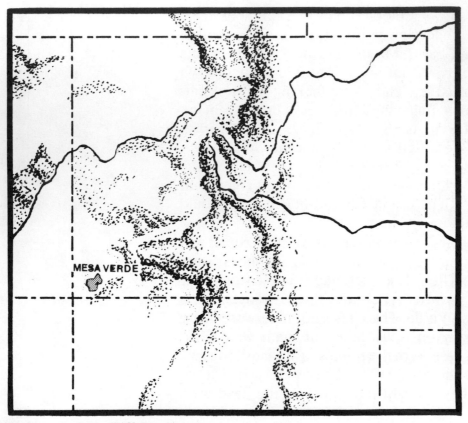

MESA VERDE

The Land of the Cliff Dwellers

For two days, the cowboys explored the mesa. First they went into the big cave. They named it Cliff Palace.

"We spent several hours going from room to room," Charlie later said.

Discovering a cliff dwelling
Courtesy *Colorado's First Portrait*

They searched for other caves and found two more. These also had many rooms. But they were not so large as the rooms of Cliff Palace. They could see many other canyons. Many of those had caves in them, too. Charlie and Richard soon forgot about the lost cattle. They rode home to tell others what they had found. They had found the silent, stone cities of the Mesa Verde.

Who were the people who lived at Mesa Verde?
What was their life like there?
Why did they leave?

Archeologists have answered many of our questions. They have found many clues at Mesa Verde. The broken jars and pottery found at Cliff Palace tell us some things. The stone tools, jewelry, and grains of corn found there tell us other things. Even the little rooms and the stone walls say things about these people of long ago.

Cliff Palace

The silent city at Cliff Palace and the other cliff dwellings were once lively places. Nearly 400 Indians had once lived at Cliff Palace. Hundreds more lived in other caves. Inside each cave were little rooms with stone walls. Each family had one room. It was used for sleeping and for storing away clothes and tools. In front of the rooms, there were open spaces where they cooked, worked, and played. This made it easy for them to visit and talk with their neighbors. The Cliff Dwellers did not need large houses. Everybody could live and work outdoors under the wide roof of the cave.

In the summer, Cliff Palace was cool and shady. It was a good place for children to play and for grown-ups to visit and talk. The men could talk about how well the corn was growing in the fields. Or they could take the older boys down into the kivas for their lessons. The

Cliff Palace

kivas were little rooms built under the ground. Each had a square hole in the roof with a ladder sticking up. Only the men and the older boys could use the kivas. There the boys were taught about the spirits that lived in the earth. They also learned about the witches that made people sick. Sometimes the medicine man took sick people to the kivas. If he had strong magic, he might make them well again. Not many people got sick during the warm summers, however.

Winters at Cliff Palace were much different. Then the cave was very cold. The Indians tried to keep warm by wearing robes and blankets. Some of the blankets were made of cotton. The warmest blankets were made of turkey feathers. Life was not easy for the turkeys. They kept losing their feathers all winter long. It also helped for the Indians to sit close to the little fires that burned every day. But the warmest place to be was down in the kivas. The little underground rooms stayed very warm, even at night. But only the men and the older boys could sleep around the little fires in the kivas. Everyone else went to bed huddled together under a pile of blankets. The winter was a bad time. Many people got sick, and some people died. But finally the winter would be over, and the warm days of spring would come again.

In the spring, Cliff Palace was a very busy place. The grown-ups had much work to do in the fields and in the cave. Children were busy playing. The older children went off down the trails to play. The boys could set snare traps. Maybe they could catch a young squirrel or a chipmunk. Even the turkeys were busy hunting for insects and growing new feathers.

The women were busier than anyone. It was their job to air out the blankets and clean the rooms. Perhaps some stones had come loose during the winter. These had to be repaired. Maybe they would put new plaster on the walls. They made plaster by mixing water with the clay they found up on the mesa. Sometimes they would paint the inside of the rooms. A woman who lived in a house at the south end of Cliff Palace painted her walls with the clay they found up on the mesa. Sometimes they would paint the inside of the rooms. A woman who lived in a house at the south end of Cliff Palace painted her walls with white plaster on top and red ochre at the bottom. She painted big red triangles around the wall where the two colors met. Another woman traced the shape of her hand on her wall nine times. Then she painted the hands red. Keeping the house fixed up was part of a woman's job.

It is easy to decorate a room the way the Cliff Dwellers did. Trace your hand on a piece of paper, paint it red, and cut it out. Make several of these. Paste them on a long sheet of paper and tape it on the wall. You can also do the same thing with triangles.

Pottery

Spring was also the time for the women to make pottery. Maybe a cooking pot, a water jar, a bowl, or a mug was broken during the winter. Many large water jars were needed for storing water. The early summer months would be hot and dry. The people at Cliff Palace had to save the water from the spring rains in the jars. The women at Cliff Palace made very fine pottery. The bowls and jugs were gray with black lines and shapes painted on them. They were very proud of these.

It was important for the girls at Cliff Palace to learn to make pottery. They began when they were very young. First they would go with their mothers to help them find some blue-gray clay. It was dug out of the

Some Mesa Verde pottery

canyon with a pointed stick. Then they brought it home to dry in the sun. Even a little girl could help her mother do this.

The older girls knew what to do next. They would help grind the clay on a flat stone. It was ground almost as fine as sand. Then some old, broken pottery was ground up to make grit. They knew why it was important to mix grit with the clay. Without it, a pot would crack when it dried. Next, they would help their mothers mix the clay and grit with water. This made a smooth, wet clay that was easy to work with. Then the mother was ready to make a pot.

First she made thin ropes of clay by rolling it on a smooth stone. Some of the little ropes were wound around in a circle and pinched together. This made the bottom of the pot. Then the sides were made with other ropes of clay. Very soon, a girl could guess what kind of pot her mother was making. It would be a bowl this time. The sides of the bowl had to be polished smooth. This was done by rubbing a smooth stone back and forth. Next the bowl was washed. Then lines and shapes were painted on. Finally the bowl was set in the sun to dry.

It was easy to tell when it was springtime at Cliff Palace. Pots were drying in the sun everywhere. Soon they would be ready to be fired. First holes were dug in the ground. Then the pots were put in and a fire built over them. The hot fire would make the pottery hard and strong. When it was time, the mothers raked the pots out of the fire. Out from the ashes came strong water jars and pretty bowls and mugs.

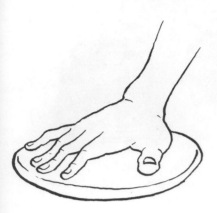

Making Pottery

Clay dirt is hard to find, but you can use clay that is already made. This is how to make a pottery bowl. First, make a flat pancake of clay.

Then make long ropes of clay.

Make the sides by laying the ropes on top of the pancake.

Then rub the walls smooth with your fingers. The clay will smooth easier if your hands are wet. Now let the bowl dry in the air for several days. Rub the bowl again inside and out until it is very smooth. Paint it with a clay slip made of fine clay mixed with water. When the slip is dry, polish the bowl by gently rubbing it with a smooth stone. The bowl is now ready to be fired in a kiln, or you can put it aside for many days to let the air dry it.

Farming

Early each spring, the men at Cliff Palace went out to the fields. Each family had a field on top of the mesa. There the Indians raised corn, beans, and squash. But first the field had to be cleared. The dead weeds were pulled up and burned. Next the ground was dug up with long pointed sticks. Some of the sticks had stone blades tied to the end. These were good digging tools. Then the field was ready to be planted.

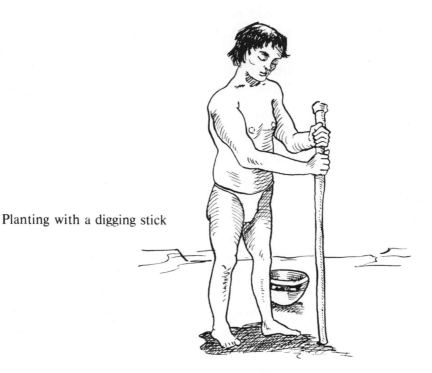

Planting with a digging stick

Planting time was decided by the Sun Watcher. He could tell the right time to plant by watching the sky. Had the birds returned from the south? This meant that summer was not far away. Each day he watched the sun set over the canyon wall. Each day it came closer to the crack in the wall. When it reached the crack it was time to plant. Each year the spring rains began soon after the sun reached the crack. The rain would soak into the dry ground and help the corn grow. Finally the day came. The Sun Watcher told the men it was now time to plant.

In a few days, the planting was finished. The seeds were in the ground waiting for the rain to come. Some years, it rained only a little. Then the people at Cliff Palace would be hungry when winter came. Some years it rained a lot. Then the people would sit in their caves watching the rain pour down. They would think of the big harvest they would have. Everyone would have plenty to eat that winter. In autumn, all the families would go up to help with the harvest. They would carry back baskets heavy with corn, beans, and squash. Sometimes the men also went hunting for deer and rabbits. But most of their food was grown in the fields.

Trading

The people at Mesa Verde made many of the things that they needed. They made their own pottery and feather blankets. They grew their own food. But some things they did not have. They did not have cotton or salt for their food. Cotton was needed to make blankets. They also needed seashells and pretty blue stones called turquoise for jewelry. To get these things, they had to go on long trips to the south.

In places farther south, friendly tribes lived. Many were also farmers who lived in stone houses. Cotton grew well in the warm country to the south. For other things, the Cliff Dwellers had to go even farther. For salt, they had to go to a big lake 200 miles away. Seashells came from the ocean. But they did not have to go all the way to the ocean for them. Seashells were traded from one tribe to the next. They also had to go far to get turquoise.

Many of the men went on the trips south to trade. Each put in his pack the things he would trade for what he needed. Maybe it was a deerskin or a new stone blade. Then they went off down the canyon. Along the way, they would visit many friendly villages. There they were treated very well. Their friends wanted to hear the news from Mesa Verde. Was the corn growing well? Had any of their old friends died? Had they seen any enemy tribes along the way? When they finished trading, the men would start out for home.

It was a special time at Cliff Palace when the men returned. Everyone gathered around. How soft the new cotton felt! Would they trade one of their seashells? The people also wanted to hear all of the news from the south. How were their friends doing? Were the enemy tribes getting closer?

They often worried about these enemy tribes. Sometimes they came to the Mesa Verde country to raid and kill. At times, they destroyed whole villages. Perhaps that was why the Mesa Verde people had moved into the caves. Once they had lived up on the mesa near their fields. But it was much safer in the caves.

The Mystery

What happened to the people at Mesa Verde? They had left their homes 600 years before the two cowboys discovered the caves. Charlie Mason thought he knew. He thought there was once a big battle at Cliff Palace. All the men were killed. Their enemies had carried off the women and the children. But Charlie was only guessing. Did he guess right? No one is sure.

What else would make hundreds of people leave their houses forever? Many people think the Indians left because they did not have enough food and water. Less and less rain fell at Mesa Verde. We know this from the trees that were growing at that time. Trees do not grow very much during dry years. We can tell this from the rings in the wood when the trees are cut down.

Cliff Palace
Photo provided by authors

In dry years, the rings are very thin. The trees tell us that Mesa Verde had very little rain for 20 years. That was about the time the people left. Without rain they would not have enough water to drink, and the corn would not grow.

Maybe the people left Mesa Verde for many reasons. But where did they go? They may have gone south. Other people very much like the Mesa Verde people lived to the south. They also lived in stone houses that were joined together. We call these people the Pueblo Indians. Maybe some of the Pueblo Indians today are related to the people who lived at Mesa Verde long ago.

Write a Book:

Would you like to make a booklet about Mesa Verde? Read the story about the Cliff Dwellers in your book over again. Decide what things you would like to have in your own book. Then decide what part should be on each page. Leave room on each page so that you can draw pictures of the things you write about.

Spruce Tree House
Photo provided by authors

Ute camps

3

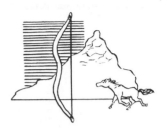

The Utes

A long time ago, the Ute Indians came to the land that we now call Colorado. They were living here long before the Spanish arrived. Some lived in the mountains and in the hills and flat lands to the south. These were the Southern Utes. The Northern Utes lived in the mountain valleys and the mesa land in the north and west. The Northern and Southern Utes were much alike and spoke the same language. But they did not often see or visit with each other. There was a high range of mountains between them; these mountains kept them apart most of the time.

The Land of the Utes

High over the land of the Utes rose the snow-capped Rocky Mountains. Between the mountains there were valleys that were green during the summer. Down into the valleys tumbled swift streams that ran fresh and clear. In some places between the mountains, there were broad, grassy lands called parks. The parks were flat areas with mountain peaks on every side. Beyond the mountains, there were rolling hills that leveled out to become the plains in the east. The mesa lands and dry, desert country were in the west. South of the mountains there were pine-covered hills and river valleys.

The Utes believed that the mountains were put there by Manitou. He was the great spirit who lived in

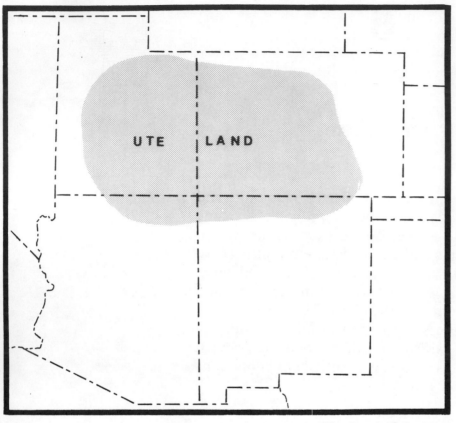

The Land of the Utes

the center of the sky. Once when he lived all alone in the sky he grew tired and lonesome and wanted to do new things. He decided to make a hole in the sky and swept out all the stones and the dirt from the floor of the sky. Then he looked down and saw great mountains which were made from the dirt and the rocks. Some of the dirt became plains, which stretched as far as he could see. Then he poured down snow and rain. To make the earth more beautiful, Manitou made the trees and flowers. Finally, he made the animals and the Utes to live in his beautiful mountains. This is why the Utes thought that the mountains were their special home.

Many kinds of animals lived in the Utes' country. On the mountain peaks high above the trees lived the bighorn sheep. They could walk along the narrow ledges and make their way up steep cliffs. Down on the sides of the mountains among the pine trees, there were elk, deer, and mountain lions. Antelope, rabbits, and beavers lived in the valleys and parks. Out on the plains were the buffalo. The Utes believed that Manitou had made all of these animals as well as the birds. He made the birds by taking handfuls of leaves and throwing them into the air. Then the leaves became birds and flew away. But the animals soon began to fight and kill each other, and that made Manitou sad. Therefore, he created the strongest animal of all to rule over all the others and to see that they lived in peace. This was the grizzly bear, the king of the beasts.

Legends are stories about how things might have happened. Can you write a story about how the grizzly bear became king of the beasts?

The Utes became a proud people feared by other Indian tribes. They often raided other Indian villages and stole their horses. The Utes were not always so strong and so feared by others; in the early days, they were a weak and peaceful tribe.

Life in the Early Times

In the early days, the Utes' life was very hard. They were not farmers. They did not grow corn and squash like the Cliff Dwellers did before them. Their food came only from the wild animals which they hunted and from wild plants and berries which they gathered.

A Ute camp in the early days

The Utes spent much of the year moving from place to place looking for things to eat. During the summer, they looked for food in the mountains. But in the winter, the valleys and mountain passes were covered with drifts of snow. Because of that, each year late in the fall they had to leave the mountains to look for food in the lower hills and valleys and sometimes on the plains. Moving from camp to camp during the winter was hard work. In the early days, they had no horses and had to carry everything on their backs. At each new camp, the men hunted while the women looked for plants and berries. They did not always find enough to eat. The Utes were often hungry during the long winter search for food.

A Ute in camp

During the winter each Ute family traveled alone. Each had its own trail down the mountain and its own berry bushes and hunting ground. Ute families then were larger than most families today. Besides the father, mother, and children, there would also be one pair of the children's grandparents and maybe an aunt, uncle, and some cousins. A family of this size was very useful. The grandparents could take care of the children when the fathers hunted and the mothers looked for food. It was important to have grandparents living with the family.

How is this different from our families today?
Which kind of family would you rather have?

Ute children

Ute mothers carried their babies on cradle boards like this

The grandparents were important also because the Utes believed that the oldest people were the wisest. At meal time, the oldest person was the first to be served. To take a drink before an older person had taken his or to speak before he did was considered to be bad manners. When it was time to move camp, it was the grandfather who would say, "We must go on to the next place. There is no more food here."

Camp life was good for the Ute children. They were often spoiled by their grandparents, who spent all day watching them and playing with them. Ute parents did not believe in spanking their children when they were bad. They thought it was enough to warn them that an evil spirit would come to get them if they were not good children. Why spank them? After all, they would not be children very long.

Everyone knew that young children would soon become older boys and girls who would begin to help the family. When a Ute girl was eight or nine, she began to learn how to help her mother search for food. The boys would learn how to hunt deer and antelope or clear a new campground for the tepees. When they were fourteen or fifteen, the boys and girls could do most of the work of a grown-up person.

A Special Time

When spring came and the last snows were falling in the mountains, the Utes prepared for a special time of the year. This was the time when each Ute band met together for the Bear Dance. The families in each of the seven Ute bands may not even have seen one another during the winter. A few of the families might have come together if they were attacked by an enemy tribe. Now before returning to the mountains, all the families in each band would meet together. It would be a happy time of visiting, dancing, story telling, and playing games. It would all begin with the Bear Dance.

Ute tepees

The Utes had a story about how they first learned the Bear Dance. They said that a man went to sleep once and had a dream. He dreamed that he would meet a bear if he went to a place in the mountains. When he woke up, he went to that place and saw a bear dancing forward and backward. The bear taught him how to do this dance and how to sing the Bear Dance song. Then the man came home and taught the dance and song to his people. Every spring after that when the bears woke from their winter sleep, the Utes met together for the Bear Dance. That was the story.

The Utes loved to dance. They danced before leaving for a new camp and before putting up their tepees when they arrived. In the early days the Bear Dance was their favorite, but they knew many other dances. They liked the Bear Dance because it lasted for three days and three nights and ended with a great feast. It was also a favorite dance of other Indian tribes, who learned it from the Utes.

You can learn it, too.

Girls should line up on the south side of the room or playground. Boys line up on the north. The two groups face each other. Then the groups start moving backward and forward in time to the music. Here's how:

1. Take two big steps forward.
2. Take three small steps backward.
3. Keep repeating these steps over and over.
4. As the girls go forward, the boys go backward. Your teacher can play the music for you.

The Utes also loved music. They had flutes made of deer bone and love flutes made of wood. The love flutes were played by the young men. They would hide

The Bear Dance

out near a girl's tepee and play the flute and sing for her. She had to guess who it was. For the Bear Dance, the Utes played the morache or rasp. This was a stick with notches cut in it. It was played by rubbing another stick over the notches. When the morache was played on a basket covering a hole in the ground, it made a very loud noise.

Would you like to make a morache?
The Utes made theirs out of cottonwood. They cut notches in a stick about two and a half feet long. You could make a small one out of soft wood. To play the morache you rub a stick or bone across it. The Utes would sing to the music.

Summer Camp

When the snow began to melt in the mountains, the Utes would return to their summer homes. They went back to their mountain valleys and parks. There the wild flowers were blooming, and the streams ran clear and cold. This was a good time of the year. They found more to eat during the summer.

Then the Utes found wild onions and small potatoes growing wild. They could also eat the fruit from the yucca plant. It was shaped like a banana and was later called the "Ute banana." They also found ripe berries, chokecherries, and grass seeds. These were sometimes dried, ground up, and mixed with other food. There were plenty of young rabbits running about from which to make stew for supper.

Yet even spring and summer had their dangers.

When the snow melted in the passes and on the mountain trails, the Utes' enemies also came to the mountain valleys. The Utes had to watch out for their enemies from the plains. The Utes fought many battles with the Plains Indians to protect their mountain homes. This was the way the Utes lived in the early days, in the days before they had horses.

Horses

Before the Spanish came to America, Indians had never seen a horse. When the Spanish came to Mexico, they brought their horses with them. Some of the towns in northern Mexico were close to the Utes' winter hunting ground. This is how the Utes found out about this strange, new animal.

The Utes saw that horses would be very useful to them. When they moved from camp to camp, the horses could carry their load. With horses they could even ride out on the plains to hunt buffalo. Then they would have plenty of food. When their enemies came to find them in the mountains, the Utes could get away quickly with fast horses. This was very important as their enemies would soon have horses, too. The Utes wanted horses very much.

How could the Utes get horses? The Spanish and the other Indians would not give their horses away. And the Utes did not have gold or silver money to buy horses. The Utes saw that they would have to trade things that they had that the Spanish wanted. Sometimes they traded meat and animal hides. But the Utes were poor Indians. Often they had only enough meat or hides for their own needs. The Utes sometimes traded their children for horses. The Spanish needed children who could learn to take care of their horses and sheep. They found that Ute children grew up to become very good horse and sheep herders.

Think about how you would feel if you were a Ute child who had been traded for a horse. Think about:
1. leaving your home,
2. living in a strange new place,
3. learning new ways and a new language,
4. learning how to ride and care for horses,
5. seeing new people and making new friends.

As the Utes got more and more horses, their way of life began to change. They hunted buffalo on the plains and had plenty to eat. With more food they could also live in larger groups. They could live with other families of their band in a big camp all year long. Sometimes the camps spread out for half a mile along a river or stream. The men hunted together while the women went out together to search for plants and berries. Life was no longer so lonesome during the winter. They also had warm buffalo robes to wear and strong buffalo hides for covering their tepees.

A Ute camp

The Utes also found a better way to get horses. With fast horses of their own, they could raid other Indian tribes and steal horses from them. They no longer had to trade their children. The Comanche Indians to the south were very rich in horses. So many of their horses were stolen by the Utes that the two tribes became bitter enemies. Sometimes the Utes also raided the Arapahoes and the Cheyennes on the plains. With horses, the Utes became a strong tribe feared by other Indians.

A Ute chief

Life in the big camps was very exciting. In the morning, one of the leaders of the band would announce what was to be done that day. Each band now had chiefs or camp leaders. Only the leaders wore bonnets made from eagle feathers with more feathers streaming down the back. A chief might announce a buffalo hunt. Sometimes the war chief would decide to lead a raid. All the men who wanted to go on the raid would get their fastest horses and join him. Sometimes the Ute women went along to tend the camp.

A Horse Raid

After many days, a Ute war party would find a Cheyenne or Comanche village with a lot of horses. The Utes would rush in and chase off as many of the horses as they could. When the Indians in the village came after them, they would try to get away as fast as they could. At times, they fought with their bows and arrows. If the Utes killed an enemy, they would scalp him and take his clothes and bow and arrows. Sometimes they would return from a raid with many things that they could use besides horses. When they arrived back in camp after a big raid, many Ute people would come out to meet them.

After a raid or a hunt, the Utes gave away what they did not need. They gave horses and clothing to the Indians who were poor. After a hunt, anyone could send a child over when fresh meat was brought in. He would sit down to wait and not say a word. Everyone knew what the child had come for. A Ute hunter always gave meat to those who needed it. Someday he might need something, too. If a man gave away many horses and much meat, he might be asked to be chief someday. It meant that he could take care of his people.

When they lived in the big camps, the Utes learned many new dances. They did not have to wait until spring for all the families to meet to have a big dance. They could dance together any time of the year. After a raid was a good time for a dance. Sometimes they did the Lame Dance. It was danced by the women, who dragged their right feet as they moved. This was to show how heavy the load was that they had carried home from the raid. They would also do the Scalp Dance or the War Dance after a raid.

This is how the Utes lived. Life was very hard at first. Then the Spanish came to Mexico with their horses. After the Utes got horses, life was much better for them. They hunted buffalo and raided enemy tribes.

Sometimes their enemy came into the mountains to raid them. Sometimes Utes would be killed in the raids and their families would be very sad. But they still had the mountains to live in during the summer and the hills and mesa land in the winter. The land of the Utes still belonged to them.

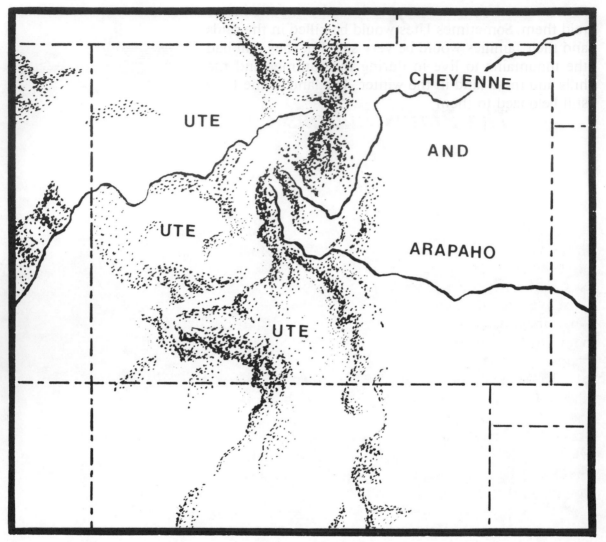

The Plains Indian Tribes
Can you tell which of the tribes on the map are
called Plains Indians? Why are not the Utes called
Plains Indians?

4

The Plains Indians

Not all of the Indians in what we call Colorado lived in the mountains as the Utes did. Some Indian tribes lived on the plains. Two of the plains tribes were the Arapahoes and the Cheyennes. Both had come here after the Utes. The Arapahoes had once lived far to the east. The Cheyennes came from the north. They had once lived in villages where they planted corn and grew what they needed. They were farmers. Both tribes began to live much differently after they came to the plains.

The Arapahoes were the first to move west to the plains. Other Indian tribes from the east had pushed them off their land. On the plains, they gave up farming and lived by hunting buffalo, deer, rabbits, and other wild animals. Berries and plants that grew on the plains could also be eaten. In those days, they did not have horses, so they had to hunt buffalo on foot.

The Cheyennes also came to the plains to live as hunters. At first, they did not have horses, and they did not live in tepees. Their houses were made of sticks covered with mud. When they moved from place to place, they had to leave their houses behind. Everything they owned had to be carried on their backs or on a travois pulled by dogs. After they had horses, they discovered how to make a new kind of house that they could take with them. This was the tepee.

The Arapahoes and Cheyennes were good friends. They would often visit each other and join together to raid enemy tribes. People from the two tribes talked to

These horses are moving the Indians' tepees. Can you find the tepees?

each other in sign language. They could not speak each other's language. They had many enemies. To the north and to the east lived the Crow and the Pawnee Indian tribes. The Arapahoes and the Cheyennes fought many battles with these tribes. The Comanches, Kiowas, and Apaches to the south were once their enemies also. After many battles with them, they made peace and after that were friendly. But they never made peace with the Utes. They often went into the mountains to steal horses from the Utes and to prove how brave they were. Being brave in battle was very important to the Arapahoes and the Cheyennes. It was part of their way of life.

The Village

The Plains Indians lived in small villages. Many families lived in each village to help protect each other and to hunt together. Each tribe had many villages or bands. In the village, the Indians put up tepees or lodges made of tall poles covered with buffalo skins. This made their homes easy to move when they went on long hunts. Some of the lodges had pictures painted on them which told about the brave things their owners had done.

This was Chief Little Raven's tepee. What can you tell about Little Raven from the pictures painted on it? What pictures would you paint on your tepee if you were an Indian?

Each morning everyone in the village woke up as soon as the sun came up. The men and boys went down to the river for a swim, while the women made breakfast. After breakfast everyone had things to do. The men went hunting or stayed at home to repair their bows and arrows. The men who were too old to hunt sat and told stories about the deer and the buffalo they had killed or about the battles they had fought. The older boys went out to look after the horses. Children played or listened to the old men's stories.

This is a picture of an Indian camp. Can you find the drying meat? Do you see the sausage?

Much work was done by the women. Some gathered berries and dug up roots to be cooked. Others cut meat into strips and placed the strips on poles to dry. Dried meat did not spoil. Sometimes they would pound up berries with the dried meat. This was called pemmican. If a very big buffalo had been killed, the women might make sausage. They would break up the big leg bones with their hammers. Then they would boil the bones for a long time. When all the fat had come out of the bones, they would put it inside of a clean buffalo intestine. They would use wild sage and wild onion to make the sausage taste good. The women also made new clothes out of deer and buffalo skins, and they cleaned the tepees.

Later in the day, the men came home with fresh meat for dinner. The women brought in the berries and the plants they had found and bundles of sticks for the fire. Soon a fire was started in each tepee and dinner was prepared. After dinner, the children played while their mothers and fathers visited and talked. Soon the sun went down and it was time for bed.

Here is a busy Cheyenne village. Can you figure out what all the people are doing? Do the people in your neighborhood get together in the evening to visit and play?

The Arapahoes and Cheyennes were proud of their tepee homes. When they later learned about houses made of wood, they did not think those were nearly as pretty. Was it not better to have a tepee with tall poles that reached up to the sky? The tepee was big enough to hold all the things the family needed. Around in a circle inside were the low beds covered with buffalo robes. They were also soft to sit on during the day. Under the beds the extra robes and clothes were stored away. In the middle of the tepee was the fire for cooking and for heating the tepee in the winter. A hole was left at the very top for the smoke to go out. A pot with something to eat was kept warm on the fire for hungry children or for visitors. It was bad manners to let a visitor leave without giving him food to eat. Bags of dried meat and fruit hung from the lodge poles up out of the way. The tepee seemed dark and cool in the summer and warm and rosy in the winter.

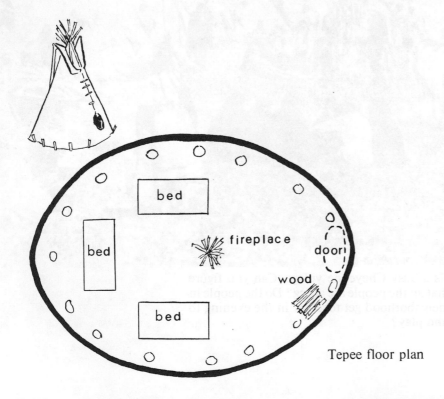

Tepee floor plan

Children

Growing up in an Arapaho or Cheyenne village was much different from growing up today. The boys and girls did not go to school. Indian children learned in a different way. When they were very young, they learned to be quiet when older people were talking. They also learned by playing games. They boys played hunting and war games with little bows and arrows. Sometimes the girls played with them, and together they made villages with little tepees. With sticks for horses the boys would pretend to go out to hunt buffalo or raid an enemy village. The girls also played with dolls made out of deer skin. They carried their dolls on their backs in little cradle boards, just as their mothers carried their babies. The girls also made clothes for their dolls. These were the things they would have to do when they became mothers. This is how their mothers and fathers had learned when they were children.

Would you like to learn to play some Indian games?
Ask your teacher to tell you how.

Their mothers and fathers and the older people in the village would also talk to them about things they needed to know. Wikis was a Cheyenne boy whose father was dead. When Wikis was ten years old, his uncle began to teach him how to act as a Cheyenne. His uncle said to him:

"When older people speak to you, you must listen to them and do as they say. You must get up early in the morning, when the sun first shines, and look for your horses. You must take care of your bow and arrows. A man with a poor bow and broken arrows cannot hunt or fight. It is important to do all these things, but most important of all is that you be brave. You must always say to yourself, 'I will be brave; I will not

A buffalo

fear anything.' Then you will always fight well and people will say you are a man."

When the children were older, they would learn other things. The boys went buffalo hunting with the men. As the girls grew bigger, they helped their mothers carry in the wood and the water. They learned how to make moccasins and how to sew beads on their dresses. Soon they would learn how to cook and how to scrape hides.

Crow Bed was a very young Cheyenne when he killed his first buffalo. He went out one day with the hunters on one of his father's best horses. Soon he was chasing the buffalo and saw a little calf that he wanted. He shot many arrows at it before the calf fell. Crow Bed was so excited that he forgot to cut it up and take the meat from the bones. The whole calf was so heavy that he could hardly get it up onto his horse.

When Crow Bed rode into his village, the people laughed at him. It was such a little buffalo. They also laughed because he had brought it all home, meat, bones, and all. But his father was proud of him. He was glad that his son had killed his first buffalo. He told him that he had done well.

"After a little while," his father said, "you will get to killing larger ones, and pretty soon you will kill big buffalo."

Wikis and Crow Bed and other Indian children learned many things without going to school. They learned how to ride horses when they were very young. Even before they could walk, the little children rode in front of their mothers on trips across the plains. Then they learned to ride the gentle, old horses and finally the young ponies by themselves. These were things they needed to know.

The Buffalo Hunt

The buffalo were very important to the Indians who lived on the plains. They liked fresh buffalo meat. Sometimes it was roasted over the fire. The women also cut up the meat to make buffalo stew. When they had more fresh meat than they could eat, it was cut into strips and dried. Sometimes it was made into pemmican.

The Indians made many things from the parts of the buffalo. From the hide they made tepee covers, robes, bed covers, and clothes. Their cups and spoons were made from buffalo horns. From the bones they made strong tools for scraping hides and for digging. Even the fat was used to make soap and the hoofs to make glue.

From spring until fall, the Indian villages were moved about from place to place following the buffalo. Women, children, and all the old people went along. They all loved to travel across the plains, making a new camp where the water was clear and the grass was green. When there were no buffalo close by, the men rode out across the plains looking for them. When they found a big herd, they would bring the good news back

shield

Things Made from the Buffalo

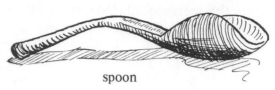

spoon

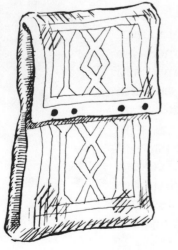

parfleche

to the village. Then it was again time for the village to move.

When they camped near a large herd, the Indians would not let a hunter go out by himself. A man hunting alone might frighten the herd and chase it away only to kill one buffalo. Then many people would go hungry. It was best for all of them to hunt together. Then everyone would have plenty to eat.

54

The buffalo hunt was an exciting time. The hunters would slowly move up as close to the herd as they could before the buffalo saw them. Then, as the herd tried to run away, the hunters would chase after it on their fastest horses. With the dust flying all around them, the men would make their kill. Some shot arrows at the buffalo. Others stuck the animals with their

These people are busy packing up to move. What do you think they have done with the skin cover for the tepee? How will they carry the long tepee poles?

lances. Either way was very dangerous. The hunter's horse and the buffalo were side by side going as fast as they could go. If the horse fell or the buffalo turned the wrong way, the hunter could be badly hurt or killed. The chase was over when they had killed all the buffalo they needed.

If the hunt was close to the camp, the women and children came out to watch and to help. The women skinned the animals and cut up the meat. Each could tell which buffalo were hers by the marks on her husband's arrows. The first time a young boy or girl came out to the hunting ground was a special time. One of the older hunters would dip his hand in buffalo blood and smear it over the child's face. The child could not wash

Riding into the herd

Driving the buffalo into a pen

it off until he was back in camp. After the buffalo were skinned, the hides and meat were taken back to camp on pack horses. Everyone had fresh meat again, and the village was happy.

This was the way the Plains Indians lived for many years. They hunted buffalo and lived in small villages. Sometimes the whole tribe would also meet together. All the Cheyennes came together once every summer.

That was a very special time. They could see all their old friends again. Some would dance the Sun Dance. Sometimes the whole tribe would go out for a buffalo hunt. Then each village would go off by itself again. The Plains Indians thought this was a good way to live.

This was their way of life. It was before any towns were built. It was before the farmers, ranchers, and miners came to build their houses. But other people were coming. They would have different ideas about how to live. They would plow up the earth and grow their food. They would kill all the buffalo and raise cattle on the plains. They would dig gold and silver out of the mountains. These people thought this was a good way to live. But how would they get along with the Indians? Both thought their way of life was the best. This would cause a lot of trouble later on.

A Plains Indian camp

Skinning a buffalo

Indian Sign Language

The first sign that an Indian child learned was the name of his tribe.

If he were an Arapaho, he would first make the sign for Indian and then the sign for mother. The word "Arapaho" means "the mother of all tribes."

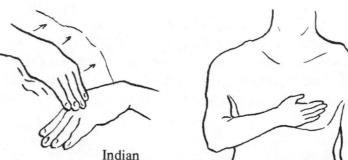

Indian

mother

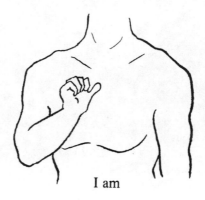

I am

The word "Cheyenne" means "finger chopper." This is the sign you would use:

A Ute had to make more signs for his name. He might make the sign for Indian, then the sign for color, and finally the sign for red. The Utes had dark skin and black hair. They were sometimes called the Black Indians, or the Black Red Men.

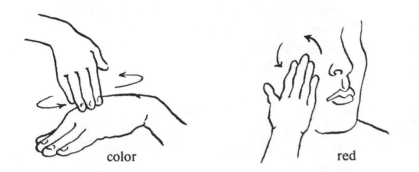

color   red

You can learn to say, "I am hungry," or "I am hot," or "I am cold." Use these signs:

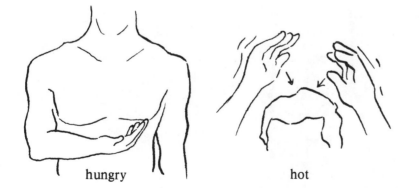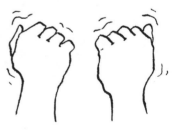

hungry   hot   cold

Mountain man ready to trap beaver

5

Explorers, Trappers & Traders

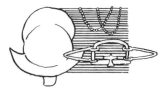

For many years, the area that we know as Colorado was the hunting ground of the Utes and the Plains Indians. But that did not last forever. In time, other groups of people would come to live here, too. Spanish-speaking people would come from New Mexico and English-speaking Americans would come from the East. Some would come to trap the beaver in the mountain streams. Others came to trade with the Indians. Later, when gold and silver were discovered, thousands of miners would cross the plains. Others would come to make farms, ranches, and towns where the Indians had once hunted. But at first, the Indians did not have to worry about these other Americans taking away their land. Not many of them knew about this land or wanted to come here.

The first of these new people to find out about this area were explorers and traders. Spanish explorers had visited it even before the Arapaho and Cheyenne Indians moved out to the plains. Spanish traders from Mexico had also made trips north to trade with the Utes and to find stolen horses. Sometimes they would buy Indian slaves from the Utes. While at first some slaves were Ute children, more often they were Indians which the Utes had captured from other tribes. In northern Mexico, they would live with the Spanish families and work for them. Some Frenchmen from Canada also traded with the Pawnee Indians who lived on the plains. They gave the Pawnees guns for their furs and buffalo robes. By the early 1800s, a few English-speaking Americans were also coming to trade with the Indians and the Mexicans.

Zebulon Montgomery Pike

Some Early Explorers of Colorado

Spanish Explorers:

Juan de Ulibarri — Many early explorers were Spanish. Juan de Ulibarri visited the plains in 1706 with 40 Spanish soldiers. He was looking for Indians who had run away from villages which the Spanish ruled. He found them and marched them back home.

Don Juan Maria de Rivera — In 1765, he explored the San Juan mountains looking for gold and silver. Other Spanish explorers came for the same reason. They did not have much luck.

Silvester Escalante — With Francisco Dominquez and eight other men, he set out in 1776 from Santa Fe to find a way to California. He crossed through what is now western Colorado but was turned back by heavy snows and winter storms.

American Explorers:

Zebulon M. Pike — The first American explorer to come here, Pike and his men came up the Arkansas River in 1806. Off in the distance, they saw a tall mountain peak that looked like a "small blue cloud." They camped at the bottom of the peak, but the snow was too deep for them to climb it. Later, people called this Pike's Peak.

Stephen H. Long — With 18 men, Major Long came here in the summer of 1820. After crossing the plains, they followed the Platte River to the mountains. A mountain peak was later named after Stephen H. Long.

At first, the Americans who lived in the eastern states knew very little about the mountains and plains. They thought of everything west of the Mississippi River as "Indian Country." They could see on their maps that part of what is now Colorado belonged to the United States. The French had sold it to the United States in 1803, when Thomas Jefferson was President. Many Americans also knew about Zebulon Pike's trip here. Pike was sent by President Jefferson to explore the area. He kept notes and later wrote a book about what he had seen. In it, he described the mountains and the plains, told about hunting buffalo and about the Indian tribes he had met. It was from Pike's book that many Americans learned about the Rocky Mountain region for the first time.

Would this area be a good place in which to live? Would Americans ever want to come here to farm and build houses and towns? Major Stephen H. Long, another American explorer, tried to answer these questions. With 18 men he crossed the plains to the Rocky Mountains in the summer of 1820. It was a hot summer, and the grass on the plains was dry and brown. In some places where the wind had piled up the sand, nothing at all was growing. When Major Long returned home, he said that Americans would never want to live there. They would not be able to farm and raise food in such a dry place. On his map he wrote the words "Great American Desert" across the plains. Surely no one would want to leave the green fields and forests of the East to live in a desert.

What is a desert?
Was Major Long correct in calling the plains the Great American Desert?

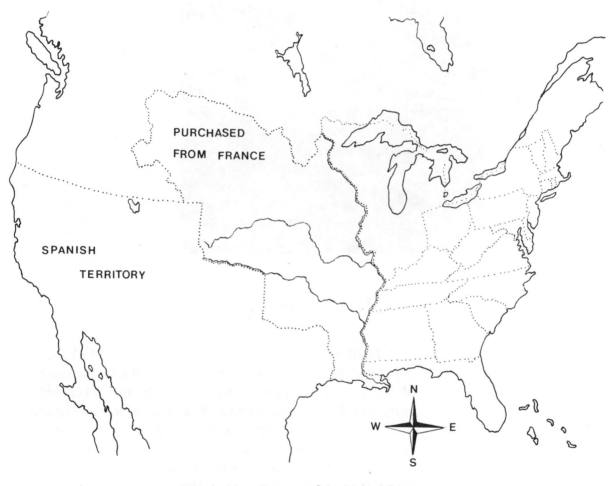

This is what the map of the United States looked like in 1803. Can you find the Mississippi River? Can you find the area that is now Colorado?

Stephen H. Long

The Fur Trappers

To most Americans in the United States of 1820, it did not matter much if the plains were a desert. Much of the good farm land in the East was still unsettled. Why should they move so far west where there were no towns and shops? "Nothing there but Indians and wild animals," they said. But some Americans were interested in Indians and in the wild animals that grew thick, furry pelts. These were the fur trappers and Indian traders.

In those days, the fur trappers were always among the first to explore the remote areas. They came up the rivers in boats looking for new trapping grounds. Sometimes they also built trading posts and bought furs from the Indians. As they came closer to the western mountains, they found that the rivers were not deep enough for boats. But that did not stop them. They set out across the plains with pack horses to reach the new trapping grounds in the Rocky Mountains. It was the fur trappers who really explored the mountains and river valleys of what is now called Colorado.

A fur trapper

In many ways, the fur trappers had learned to live like the Indians. They lived off the land, hunting deer, antelope, and buffalo for food. Wearing Indian-type moccasins and deerskin clothes, they dressed very much like the Indians. At night, they rolled up in buffalo robes to go to sleep. Because their hair was long and their faces brown from the sun and wind, it was sometimes hard to tell if they were trappers or Indians.

The trappers came mainly to trap the beavers that lived in the icy water of the high mountain streams.

There in the middle of the streams, the beavers built their houses of sticks and mud. It was the safest place they could find. To make it even safer, they dammed up the streams with small trees cut down with their sharp front teeth. This made a pond around their house and kept the entrance under water. In time of danger, they could dive under the water and swim into their houses. Their webbed hind feet made the beavers good swimmers. By slapping the water with their broad, flat tails, they could also warn other beavers of danger. When the cold weather came, the beavers grew thick, glossy coats of fur. This kept them warm in the winter. It also brought the greatest danger of all — the fur trapper.

In the fall of each year, the trappers set out for the beaver ponds in the mountains. They set their traps in the fall and again in the spring when the beaver fur was thick. Each beaver pelt that they brought back was worth six to eight dollars. The pelts were sent to the eastern cities and to Europe, where the fur was made into fine, tall hats for men.

The trappers sometimes went out alone, but more often in small groups. Together they could protect themselves from unfriendly Indians. Each carried a heavy gun that could kill a grizzly bear or a buffalo. Over his saddle he hung a "possibles bag." It held all the little things a trapper might possibly need, like flint and steel, needles and thread, and lead for making bullets. The pack horse carried the larger things, such as traps, bed rolls, and knives to trade with friendly Indians. When they reached the mountains and found signs of beaver, the trappers would stop to make camp.

Possibles bag

Fur trappers carried things they needed in their possibles bag. If you were going camping over night, what would you bring in your possibles bag?

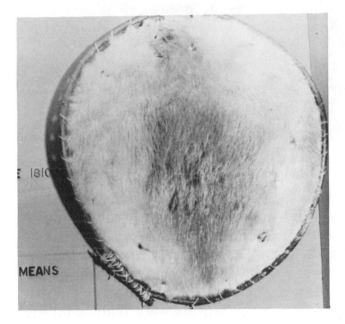

Can you tell the story of how this hat was made?

A beaver dam

A beaver

In the afternoon, the trappers waded up the stream to set their traps. They knew the ways of the beaver. They knew that beavers liked the smell of other beavers. Near each trap set under the water, the trappers put beaver scent. During the night, a beaver might swim over to see what was there and be caught by the trap. Early the next morning, the trappers would check their traps. Any unlucky beavers were skinned on the spot, and their pelts were taken back to camp. Then the trappers would scrape the skins clean and stretch them over a willow tree to dry. After a day or two of trapping, they would move on to make a new camp.

Winter came early in the mountains, and the trappers had to work fast. Soon the snow would be deep in the passes, and the cold blizzards would blow. Some trappers would then go back down the rivers to the trading posts on the plains. Others would find their way to the lower valleys and spend the winter in a log cabin. The next summer, men from the trading posts would bring fresh supplies out to them. By fall, they would be deep in the mountains again, trapping beavers. So the years passed.

Fur trapping in the mountains could not last forever. By the 1840s, most of the beavers were gone. Anyway, the men in the East and in Europe decided that they liked silk hats better than beaver hats. They stopped buying hats made of fur, and the price of beaver pelts fell. Trapping a beaver was hardly worth the effort after that. The fur trappers had to find other things to do. Some settled in the river valleys and became farmers. Some became guides for people going west. Others went to live in Mexico. Later, during a war with Mexico, some became scouts for the Army. They helped lead the Army troops across the mountains which they knew so well.

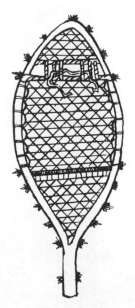

Snowshoes

Kit Carson

When he was sixteen, Kit Carson ran away from home. He went with Charles Bent on a trading trip to Santa Fe. There he met many mountain men and decided that he wanted to be a fur trapper. Because he was so small, many people did not take him seriously. Kit never grew to be a very big man in size, but he became one of the best fur trappers in the West. He was also a scout for the army and fought in many battles with the Indians. He joined the army during the Civil War and was commander at Fort Garland. Kit lived in Taos, New Mexico, much of his life, but returned to Colorado to retire. He died at Fort Lyons in 1868, and his last words were "Adios, compadre," or "Goodbye, friend." Kit was everyone's friend.

Jim Beckwourth

As a mountain man and army scout, Jim Beckwourth led a very exciting life. He had dangerous fights with wild animals. The Indians almost killed him in several battles. But Jim also lived with the Indians of the Crow tribe. They even made him a chief. Jim was also a beaver trapper and an Indian trader. For a while he lived on a farm near Denver. In 1866, when he was sixty-eight years old, Jim was asked by the government to visit the Crow Indians to try to get them to stop fighting. Jim never came back. No one knows for sure what happened. Most people believe that the Crows fed Jim poisoned meat. When he had lived with them before, he had brought them good luck. The Crow tribe wanted to keep him with them forever — dead or alive.

The Santa Fe Trail

The fur trappers were not the only Americans who came west in those days. Others came to trade with the Indians and with the people who lived in northern Mexico. They found that the best place to trade was Santa Fe, a town in northern Mexico. When Mexico had belonged to Spain, Americans were not allowed to trade there. The Spanish were afraid that the Americans would try to make northern Mexico part of the United States. When the Mexican people became independent from Spain in 1821, they let the Americans come. Santa Fe was so far north of other Mexican cities that it was hard to trade with them. The American towns in the East were closer.

At first there was no road to Santa Fe. The American traders had to find their way across the open plains. But soon the wagons that left each summer made a trail across the plains that others could follow. This was known as the Santa Fe Trail. It crossed part of what is now Colorado. The traders who drove their wagons along the Santa Fe Trail learned more about this region. They found out which Indian tribes along the way were friendly and which would try to raid the wagons to steal guns and horses. Although it was very dry in the summer, they learned where to find water for themselves and their horses. And they learned more about the people of northern Mexico.

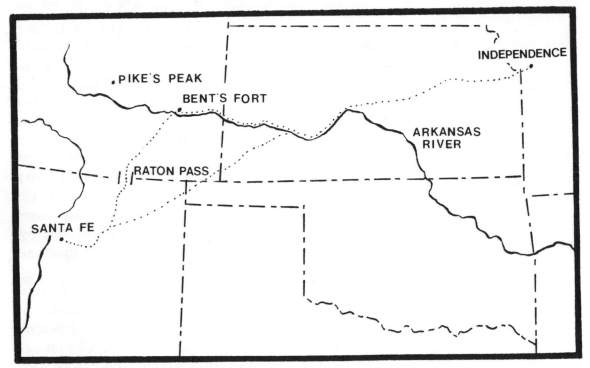

Can you find the Santa Fe Trail on the map? What part of the area that is now Colorado did it cross?

The people of Santa Fe were glad to see the first wagons come each summer. It meant that the stores would again be filled with things the people needed. The traders also liked Santa Fe. They liked many of the Mexican customs, such as the fandangos or dances held in the town plaza. The plaza was the open square in the center of town. Some American traders stayed and opened their own stores in Santa Fe. In time, many Americans would live there. Many learned to speak Spanish, and some married Mexican women.

Bent's Fort

In 1829, two brothers, William and Charles Bent, came to Santa Fe. They had once worked for the fur trading posts in the East. That was before they found out that Americans were trading at Santa Fe. In Santa Fe, they opened a store with Ceran St. Vrain, an old friend of theirs from the East. The three men decided they could make more money if they worked together. Ceran St. Vrain would tend the store while Charles Bent brought more wagons filled with goods from the East. But what would William Bent do? Just twenty years old, William was a young man full of energy. He could not find enough to do in Santa Fe to keep busy. Sometimes he went off to trade with the Indians. He got to know many of the Arapahoes and Cheyennes and came home with many stories about them.

This gave the Bent brothers and St. Vrain an idea. William liked the Indians who lived on the plains, and they liked him. He had once saved two Cheyenne braves from a group of Comanches. The Cheyennes would always remember that William Bent was their friend. Why not build a trading post on the plains where William could spend his time trading with the Arapahoes and the Cheyennes? They could bring in buffalo robes to trade for knives, beads, iron pots, and other things they might need. It was a very good idea, indeed.

The trading post which they built on the Arkansas River looked more like a fort than a store. Bent's Fort, as it was called, was a large rectangle with four high walls. It was made of sun-dried bricks called adobes. The only opening in the walls was a heavy wooden door that could be closed in case of an attack. Above the walls rose two look-out towers. Inside the walls on the ground floor there were store rooms, living rooms and work rooms. Other living rooms were built on the second floor. The traders could also work in the large open space in the center. Here they could press the buffalo robes into tight bundles, repair their wagons, and load them. A closed-in area for the horses and oxen was built onto the fort in the back.

The news that William Bent had built a great trading fort on the Arkansas spread quickly across the plains. Many Arapahoes and Cheyennes came to visit the fort, putting up their tepees nearby. Bent explained his plans to them. He had many useful things to trade for their buffalo robes. They should get ready. As soon as the weather turned cold, the traders would visit their villages.

Bent's Fort

Trade Goods

These were some of the things the traders brought out to trade with the Indians.

lead	axes	beads
cloth	iron	wire
knives	pots	kettles
	blankets	

Why do you think the Indians wanted these? Could they have made them?

With the snow falling and the ground frozen hard, the traders set out from Bent's Fort. Winter was the busy trading season. By then, the buffalo had grown thick and heavy robes. These were the best. With loaded carts or pack horses, the traders went to the Indian villages. Everyone came to look at the trade goods spread out on the floor of the chief's tepee. There were Navaho blankets; white, blue and red beads; iron for making arrowheads; iron pots and kettles; and axes and knives. Next they had to agree upon the price. For a fine Navaho blanket, an Indian might have to give as many as ten buffalo robes. When the trading was finished, the traders loaded up and went off to find another village.

In the spring, wagon loads of buffalo robes left Bent's Fort for the East. The robes were sold in the towns in Missouri. The traders bought a new supply of trade goods with the money. The wagons filled with trade goods came back to the fort in the summer. Then William Bent was ready for another trading season. It continued like that for many years.

During these years of trading, many different people learned to live together. Indians, Mexicans, and Americans from the East learned each other's customs.

Many of the American traders married Indian and Mexican women. William Bent married a Cheyenne named Owl Woman. His brother Charles married Ignacia, a Mexican woman. Sometimes there was fighting and war between the different people in the West. Some people were killed. But many others lived together in peace during these years.

A fur trader

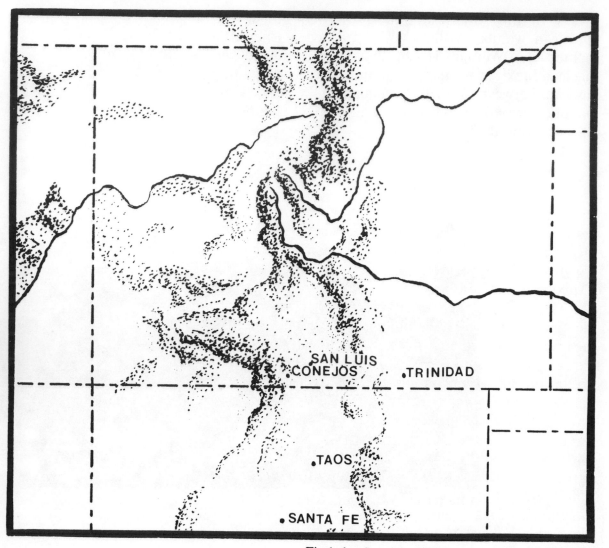

Find the Spanish-American towns on this map.
Have you been to any of these towns?

6

The Spanish-Americans

In the 1850s some new settlers came to live in what is now Colorado. They were Spanish-Americans who lived in the Territory of New Mexico. They are called Spanish-Americans because many early settlers in New Mexico came from Spain. Some of the people in New Mexico Territory needed more land for farming. For a long time, they had been looking to the north for a place to live. Beyond their small, crowded villages was the broad, open San Luis Valley. It was surrounded by beautiful snow-capped mountains. There was also good land east of the valley near the Purgatory River.

Twice before, groups of settlers had tried to make a new home in the valley. Each time, they had been driven back by the Utes who wanted it as their hunting ground. Then, in 1851, a little group of pioneers tried once more. The United States Army was building a fort in the San Luis Valley. The soldiers had promised to keep the Indians away, but the new settlers knew there was still danger from the Utes. They pushed on anyway. They called their new settlement San Luis. It was the first of many towns founded by the Spanish-Americans.

The Spanish-Americans spoke Spanish. Here are some words they would have used:

montaña — mountain   cielo — sky
rio — river   tierra — land
valle — valley   casa — house

It was a great adventure to make the trip north. Each group of settlers might have 20 wagons or two-wheeled carts. These would be loaded with all the clothing, cooking pots, tools, and toys that they would hold. The wagons were pulled by strong oxen. Behind the wagons came all the animals that belonged to the families. There would be herds of horses, flocks of sheep and goats, herds of cattle, and finally at the very end came the pigs. Most of the men walked along beside the different herds of animals. Sometimes they would ride horses or burros. The women and the young children would walk most of the time. When they got tired, they would ride in the wagons.

A two-wheeled cart

A wagon train this large stretched out across the land for two or three miles. It was a very slow way to travel. Sometimes the trip took a whole month. At night, the families camped in a circle. Afraid of the Indians, they made fires at night just long enough to cook their food. Somebody usually stayed awake at night to keep watch for the Indians.

Have you ever moved to a new
home?
What if you had to go in a wagon?
What would you take? What
would you leave behind?

The people tried to hurry. They needed to get to
their land before the winter snows came. But the pigs
were very slow. They wanted to sit and rest all the time.
The men would poke them and even kick them to get
them to move, but pigs can be very stubborn. The
leader of one wagon train, Felipe Baca, became very angry with the pigs. Finally he said, "My friends, we cannot wait; time is too precious now. I have got a plan by
which we won't loose [lose] them altogether. Go ahead
and give those tired fellows a blow on the head, and we
will eat them — and why not?"

As soon as they arrived at their new home, the
people stopped to pray. They were thankful that they
had lived through such a dangerous trip. What words
would they have used? "We have safely arrived at our
land. We give thanks to Saint Joseph for carrying us
through so many dangers. With the grace of God, we
shall build our new town here." But they would have
said it in Spanish.

Pretend that you have just ended
this wagon trip. Write a letter to
your friends back home. Tell them
what the trip was like.

The Villages

Sometimes the settlers were from one big family.
Each family group was large. It would include the father
and mother and the married sons with their wives and
children. There would also be younger boys and girls.

Statue of a saint

The children had many cousins to play with. Sometimes there was also an old great-grandmother or great-aunt or great-uncle in the group.

If the settlers were all from one family, they often named their village after themselves. One village was called Los Cordova. It meant: This is the Cordovas. At other times, several families would go together. Then they would name the village for the most important family or for a favorite saint. The village of San Luis was named for Saint Louis. Sometimes the settlers just thought up a name.

Here are the names of three other villages:

Conejos, Costilla, Trinidad

Can you find out what these names mean?

The first houses were called *jacales*. These were log cabins with the logs set upright instead of sideways. The spaces between the logs were filled with mud. These houses kept out most of the wind and rain, but they were not very good houses. As soon as the fields were planted, the people built better houses.

The better houses were made of adobe. Adobe is made by mixing clay and straw with water and shaping it into bricks. After they have dried in the sun, the bricks become very strong. The walls were very thick. This made the houses warm in the winter and cool in the summer. These were the kind of houses the people had lived in before they moved. They were also good houses for their new homes.

The first settlers built their houses close together in a little village, which the Spanish-Americans called a *plaza*. In some villages the houses were joined together with an open space or *patio* in the middle. During the daytime, the women used the *patio* for outdoor cooking. It was also a safe place for the children to play. At night, the men herded the cattle and sheep into the *patio*.

Building an adobe house

When the strong wooden gates were closed, the animals would be safe from wolves or from an Indian raid. The young men would lead the animals back to the pasture the next morning. In other villages, each family lived in a house with a little *patio* of its own. In the early days, the houses needed to be built strong and close together. The people could never tell when they might be attacked by the Utes.

Plaza settlement

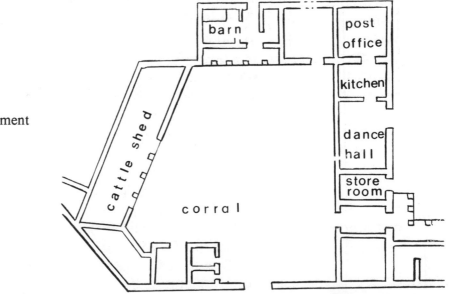

A Spanish- American village

After the Utes left the area, the Spanish-Americans built other kinds of settlements. The houses were built farther apart, often on long, narrow strips of land. These were called long-lot or ribbon settlements. The houses and the corn fields were on the front part of the lot next to a stream or river. In this way each family would be close to the water needed for their crops. The families also needed water for cooking, bathing, and washing clothes. Being close to a river or stream was very important in this dry land.

The houses were usually built close to the river. Behind the houses were the gardens and the farm lands. Here the farmers would grow such things as beans, chilies, corn, and wheat. The pastures for the animals were behind the farm. Most of this land was open to anyone to use for grazing sheep or cows. The people also shared the land toward the mountains where there were trees. Everybody needed the wood from the trees. They used it for firewood. They also used it to make furniture and tools.

84

The ribbon settlements looked like this

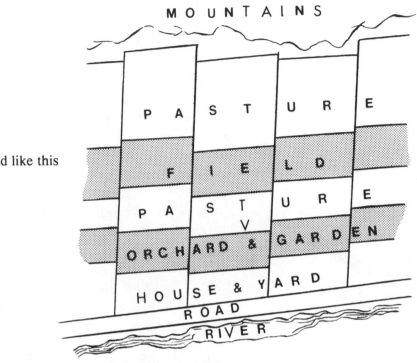

What are these burros carrying?

As there were few stores, the people had to make most of the things they used. Most people had only a few benches and tables for furniture. Their beds were mattresses made from the wool of the sheep. In the daytime, these were rolled up and kept on a bench made of adobe. The floors of the houses were made of hard-packed dirt. They were swept often and kept very clean. Sometimes the women made rag rugs for the floors.

The women also made all of the clothes for their families. They would make cloth from the wool of the sheep. They would use hides from the deer and the buffalo that the men shot. Some of the men wore suits made of deerskin. Other men wore suits made of wool. They often wore a *tilma* as a kind of overcoat. The boys dressed just like the men.

The women and girls wore long wool dresses or skirts and blouses. Sometimes they wore shawls over their heads and shoulders. All of the people wore moccasins. In the winter, they wore overshoes made of sheepskin with the warm wool next to the skin.

Why do you think they made their own clothes?

Daily Life

The men spent their days farming, herding the animals, and hunting. Farming was very hard work. The tools these early settlers had were not very good. They had very little iron or steel. Sometimes they only had wood and animal hide to make tools. Their plows and many other tools were made out of wood.

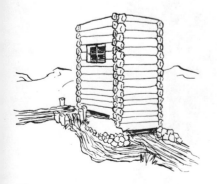

The people were very glad they had brought the oxen with them on their long trip. These strong animals would help the farmers in many ways. They pulled the wooden plows through the ground. They also pulled the carts which brought the grain from the fields. After the grain was spread out on the ground, the oxen would walk around and around to thresh it. Their heavy feet

A farmer plowing

would knock the rough outside husk off the grain. Sometimes they were even used as power to run the grist mills that made wheat into flour. Most people used water wheels for their mills if they could. The oxen were needed for other things.

How do you get the things you need to eat?
Take a piece of wood with a pointed end and see if you can plow up the ground with it.

The women and the girls also worked very hard. Cooking took up much of their time. Before grist mills were built, they had to grind the corn into meal to make tortillas or *atole*. *Atole* is a thick mush made from blue corn meal. They did this with a mano and metate that worked in the same way that the grist mills did. The women had to make candles. They also had to make their own soap. At least once a year, they put fresh plaster on the inside of their houses. From early spring until late fall when the crops were harvested, everybody worked very hard. there was little time for fun.

Much of the work in a Spanish-American village was shared. Sometimes the whole village would work together. In the spring the men went out to plant the fields together. After one field was planted, they all moved on to the next. At harvest time they divided the grain so that each family got its share. If a man was sick and not able to work, his family still got its share of the grain. At harvest time the women of the village shared the work of baking bread. If the village did not have a grist mill, the strongest women ground up the grain into flour. Other women mixed the flour with water to make dough. The older women took care of the ovens in which the bread was baking. Working together the women baked enough bread to last the village for a year. They baked it in a special way. As time went by the crust on the outside got very hard, but the bread inside stayed fresh and soft.

A family at work

Make a list of all the things that the men and boys had to do in the summer. Make a list of all the things the women and girls did. Then put a check mark beside those things on your list that you or somebody in your family does. Did you make any check marks?

Winter was a good time for these Spanish-American settlers. There was little work to do. This was a time to rest and to play. If it was warm enough, the old men would gather in the *patio* or in somebody's yard. They would sit and talk. The younger men would play games. They liked horse races and foot races. They also liked to wrestle and to play team games.

One of the team games was *el chueco*. The name came from the crooked or bent club used. The club was long enough to reach the player's waist. The ball was made of two pieces of cow or deerskin. They would sew these together over water-soaked wool. When the wool would dry, it would get larger and become very hard. Any number of people could play this game. The players would scratch a line on the ground. Half of the players would stand on each side of the line facing each other. The ball was put on the center of the line. Both sides would try to hit the ball with their *chuecos*. They would try to get it as far away from the starting line as they could. They wanted to keep it on the other team's side. All the players would agree on a time for the game to finish. Whichever side had the ball on the other team's side when the time was up would win.

When it was cold, the children would play in the house. They might play with tops that their fathers had carved out of blocks of wood. Sometimes the boys would play *juegos de la bolita*, or marble games. The girls often played with their dolls.

Ask your teacher for the directions for playing some Spanish-American games.

Holidays or *fiestas* were special times. Most of them were held to honor the saints. There are many saints, so there were many fiestas. The first one each year came on New Year's Eve. Everyone in the village would go to Midnight Mass at the church. While it was still dark the next morning, men would go around the village singing the song *Los Dias*. This means "The Two Days," the last of the old year and the first of the new year.

Christmas Eve was also a special time. In the early days, the *agüelo* (abuelo or grandfather) would go to all the houses where there were children. If they had not been good, and had not said their prayers, he would crack a whip around their legs. Then they would say their prayers and give the *agüelo* sweets. After that, they would dance around him and sing. Later on, this changed. The children became the ones who were given the sweets. They liked this must better than the old way.

Roman Catholic Church, Guadaloupe

Even when there was not a fiesta, there were happy times. Sometimes there would be storytelling in the evenings. Sometimes the father or mother would read out loud to the children. Sometimes the whole family would tell riddles. Many evenings were spent making up new words to old songs.

Here is a song in Spanish that you can learn. You may already know the tune.

Uno, dos, tres niñitos
Cuatro, cinco, seis niñitos
Siete, ocho, nueve niñitos
Diez niñitos son.

Uno, dos, tres niñitos
Cuantos son? Tres niñitos;
Cuatro, cinco, seis niñitos.
Don los buenos dias.

Seite, ocho, nueve niñitos;
Cuantos son? Nueve niñitos;
Mas uno, sondiez niñitos;
Y don los buenos dias.

Somos los diez niñitos
Nueve, ocho, siete, niñitos
Seis, cinco, cuatro niñitos
Tres, dos, uno, Adios!

See if you can figure out what the words in this song mean.

See if you can learn some other songs in Spanish.

The villages were busy and happy places in which to live. Even though the people had to make most of the things they ate, wore, and used, they still had fun.

How many of the children in your class can speak Spanish and English?

Make some labels for the things in your classroom.
Make the labels in both Spanish and English.
Tape the labels on the things in the room.
See if you can learn two of these words each day.

Here are some things you might find in your school:

desk-escritorio
clock-reloj
chalk-tiza
paper-papel
bookcase-amario para libros

teacher-maestro, maestra
calendar-calendario
window-ventana
door-puerta
pencil-lapiz

Miners depended on burros.

7

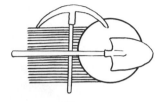

The Gold Rush

In the early summer of 1858, more than a hundred men were getting ready to cross the plains. William Green Russell and his two brothers had started out from the state of Georgia. Other Georgia men joined them. In the Indian Territory, a Cherokee Indian named John Beck loaded his wagon for the trip west. He and some of his friends met the Georgia people and rode west with them. Other men were leaving from the states of Missouri and Kansas. They, too, were headed west.

Many Americans from the East had crossed the plains before. But these men were different. They were not going to trade with the Plains Indians or the Spanish-Americans at Santa Fe. They were not going to trap beaver. These men had another reason for going west. They were going to look for gold.

They hoped to find gold in the streams and creeks along the Rocky Mountains. Maybe they would find enough to make them rich. Gold was a precious metal. A few ounces of gold was worth a lot of money. When they sat around their campfires at night, the men must have talked a lot about gold. Was it really true that the Arapaho Indians made bullets out of gold? That was a story which the trappers and Indian traders liked to tell, but John Beck had the best story of all. They liked to listen to it because they knew it was true.

Eight years before, John Beck and some other Cherokees had crossed the plains. They were on their way to California. Gold had been discovered there. Thousands of people set out for California, hoping to get rich. When they reached the Rocky Mountains, the Cherokees had stopped beside a creek. In the sand of the creek bed, one of the men with them found a little bit of gold. His name was Lewis Ralston. Maybe there was more gold nearby. The Cherokees did not stay long enough to find out.

When the men reached the Platte River, they began to look for gold. For two weeks, they searched along the creeks that flowed into the river. They looked carefully along Ralston Creek, named after the man who had discovered gold there. They found only a few specks of gold. After two weeks they had still found almost nothing. Why look any farther? John Beck, all the Cherokees, and most of the other men gave up and started for home. Only William Green Russell and 12

Denver, 1859

others stayed to look a little longer. Shortly after the other men had left, Russell and his friends found what they were looking for. They discovered gold in a stream called Dry Creek.

The men spent the rest of the summer panning for gold. Other people came to join them, for the news of the gold discovery spread quickly. Some Indian traders on their way east stopped to visit and took some gold dust back east with them. Soon the newspapers in the big eastern cities told their readers about the discovery of gold. "Go to Cherry Creek and get rich," they said. Many of the gold seekers were camped along the banks of Cherry Creek, where the city of Denver would later be. It was too late in the year for many people to try to cross the plains then. The winter blizzards would make the trip too dangerous. But the next spring, thousands of people headed west to look for gold.

The Pike's Peak Gold Rush

In the towns in Kansas and Missouri, no one could remember anything like it. It was the spring of 1859, and thousands of people were coming from the East. They were on their way to the gold diggings. All the stores were busy selling boots, shovels, hats, picks, pans, and things needed for mining gold. People set out across the plains in wagons, on horses, and some on foot, pushing little carts. They talked and dreamed about the gold they would find. This was the beginning of the Pike's Peak gold rush.

Why was it called the Pike's Peak gold rush? No one had discovered gold at Pike's Peak itself. But the people needed a name for the place where gold was discovered. When they looked at their maps, they saw that it was not far from Pike's Peak. Many people knew about Pike's Peak. So the "Fifty-Niners" used that name for the entire region. They are called Fifty-Niners because the gold rush took place in the year 1859.

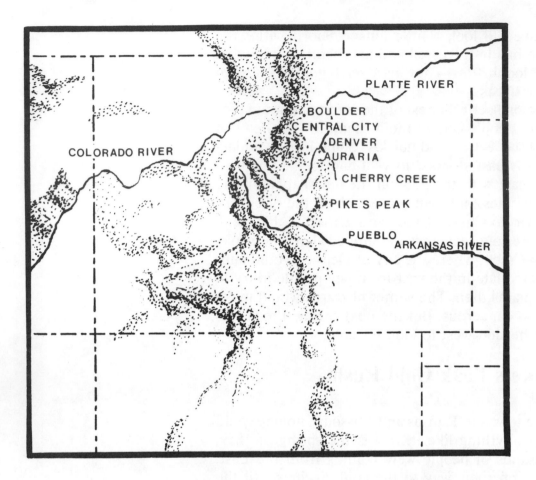

During that summer, nearly 50,000 people came to the Pike's Peak region. They were farmers, storekeepers, Indian traders, and miners. Most of them had a lot to learn about gold and where to find it. They had to learn that gold was formed millions of years ago in cracks in the hard rock of the mountains. Some of the rock crumbled into dirt and sand over the years. When it rained, the dirt and sand washed down into the creeks and rivers, taking little bits of gold with it. Sometimes it was just a tiny flake or a speck of gold dust; sometimes it was a larger nugget. So the Fifty-Niners learned that gold could be found either in the mountains or in the streams.

They would also learn the different ways of mining gold. The gold that had washed down into the streams was the easiest to get. It was called placer gold. Placer gold was mined by digging up sand and gravel from the stream beds and mixing it with water in a shallow pan. Slowly moving the pan back and forth, the miner let the rocks and dirt spill over the side. The heavier gold settled to the bottom. Sometimes the sand and gravel were shoveled into a box with water running through it. Then only the fine dirt that settled to the bottom of the box was washed in the pan. The gold that was still in the mountains was much harder to mine. It was called lode gold. Most of the lode gold was still part of the hard quartz rock of the mountain. It had to be dug out with picks and shovels or blasted out with dynamite. Then the rock had to be crushed into fine pieces before the gold could be taken out.

Panning for gold

Finding gold was not as easy as many Fifty-Niners thought. Only the first to arrive found much gold in the streams. At first, each pan might have 25¢ to 50¢ worth of gold in it. But that did not last long. The placer gold was nearly gone. Soon a man could work all day and make only a few cents. Had they come a thousand miles only to find a few cents worth of gold? Many of the miners gave up and returned home. Then good news came. Some of the miners had discovered gold in the mountains.

One of the miners from Georgia, John Gregory, made a great discovery. He found a rich lode of gold in a narrow valley or "gulch" up in the mountains. In three days, he had dug out nearly $2,000 worth of gold. And there was more where it came from. Gregory could hardly believe that he had been so lucky. "My wife will be a lady and my children shall be educated," he said, thinking about his new fortune.

When the news of Gregory's good luck reached Cherry Creek, thousands of people rushed to the mountains. Some went to Gregory's Gulch. Others followed the creeks and Indian trails deep into the Rockies. They went on horseback or on foot, leading burros loaded with the things they needed. Many of the prospectors came home tired and empty-handed, but some were as lucky as John Gregory. They found not only gold, but also silver, lead, and other metals. The Rocky Mountains quickly became famous for its rich mines.

Sluice box

What is this miner carrying on his burro?
What do you think is in the box?

The Mining Towns

Each new discovery brought a wave of miners rushing into the area. Mining camps with tents and cabins sprang up almost over night. Sometimes the camp would grow into a new town, with stores, shops, and hotels. Central City, Blackhawk, and Nevadaville grew up in Gregory's Gulch. Mining towns were started in many places. Some still exist today. Others became "ghost towns" after the gold or silver was mined out. The miners moved on to another place, leaving an empty town behind them.

The main street of a new mining town was a busy place. It was lined with stores, shops, cafes, and saloons. It was often crowded with miners who had come into town. If his pick or shovel broke, the miner could have it fixed at the blacksmith shop, or he could buy a new one at the general store. While he was there, he might

Mine shaft

also buy a new shirt, a pair of boots, or groceries. Sometimes the storekeeper would give him flour, meat, and potatoes. But the miner would then have to agree to give the storekeeper a share of the gold he might find. If he had already found gold, he could leave it at the bank where it would be safe. If he had enough money, he might eat dinner at a cafe and sleep overnight at the hotel. Before going back to work, the miner could stop at a saloon to meet with his friends.

At first, most of the people in a new mining camp were men. Many of them were young men who did not yet have families. It was easy for them to leave home to go looking for gold. The married men often left their wives and children at home. After a while, women and children could also be seen in the mining towns.

The women did not become miners, but they had a lot of work to do. They took care of their families. They baked bread and pies for the men, washed clothes for

Miners' cabin

Once the mountains above Central City were covered with trees.

What do you think happened to them?

the men, and took care of miners who were sick. Women who could sew well made new shirts or coats for the miners who could not afford to buy them at the store.

Anne Ellis was six years old when her family moved to the mining town of Bonanza. They lived in a three-room house — a kitchen and two bedrooms. On winter evenings the family sat in the front bedroom because it had a stove to keep them warm. The children liked to sit around the stove listening while their father read stories to them. When they were older, they went to school to learn how to read.

Anne's school was a building that had once been a store. As there were no desks, the children sat on benches made of lumber. Two students sat at each bench. They learned reading and arithmetic.

Christmas was Anne's favorite time of the year. Then she would help her family decorate a Christmas tree. But they did not have electric lights in those days.

Clara Brown was a freed slave. She used the money she made doing laundry in Central City to bring other black people who had been slaves out to the West. She also helped to start the first Sunday School in this area.

Bonanza, Colorado

A school in
Leadville

Instead, they made tiny candles by dipping a string into hot grease.

In the summer, Anne kept busy helping her mother. Sometimes she went into the mountains to pick berries for making jelly. Anne also helped to make ice cream. Getting the ice was her job. She walked to one of the nearby mines and asked a miner to bring up a chunk of ice. The ice came from water that had frozen deep inside the mine. It was the only place to get ice in this little mining town during the summer.

Do you help your mother the same way Anne did?
What do you do that is different?

Down on the plains, other towns sprang up. The gold seekers who arrived in 1859 found two little towns already started along Cherry Creek. The miners who had spent the winter there had laid out streets and built log cabins. One town was named Auraria, the other Denver. Later the towns were joined together to become the city of Denver. Boulder, Golden, and Pueblo were other little towns at the foot of the mountains. These were the supply towns which the mining region needed.

Supplying the Miners

Keeping the miners supplied with the things they needed was a big job. They needed tools, machines, food, and clothing. In the East, railroads and steamboats were used to bring these things to the people. Railroads did not yet come this far west, and none of the rivers were deep enough for steamboats. The only way to get supplies to the Rocky Mountains was by wagons.

Each spring, thousands of supply wagons set out across the plains. They were pulled by horses, mules, and slow-moving oxen. It often took six to eight weeks for the heavy wagons to cross the plains. These wagons were much too heavy to go up the steep roads into the mountains. This is one of the reasons why the supply

Supply wagons in Denver

towns were needed. The wagons could be unloaded there. Later the supplies were loaded on pack horses and smaller wagons. Then they were sent to the storekeepers in the mining towns.

The biggest problem was keeping the miners supplied with food. Sometimes they killed buffalo and deer for meat, but they were not used to eating roots and berries as the Indians did. The miners wanted bread made from flour. They liked potatoes, beans, and other kinds of vegetables. Sometimes they could get grain and vegetables from the Spanish-Americans who lived toward the south. But most of what they needed had to come across the plains in wagons. The men who owned the wagons charged very high prices. It cost the miners a lot of money just to be able to eat.

Some of the Fifty-Niners decided that they could make a good living by growing food for the miners. One of these men was David Wall. When he came to the Pikes Peak region in 1859, he brought some garden seed with him. He found some good land along one of the creeks. There was only one problem. Not enough rain fell each summer for garden plants to grow. But David Wall knew how to solve that problem.

Once he had taken a trip to California, where the summers were also very dry. He had seen the farmers there bringing water to their fields. They had learned from the Spanish in California to dig a ditch to the nearest stream. By opening the ditch the farmers could give the plants water when they needed it. The Spanish had farmed this way for many years. Even some Indian tribes had farmed this way. It is called irrigated farming.

That summer, David Wall planted a big garden. He raised potatoes and many kinds of vegetables. His ditch from Clear Creek brought all the water that he needed. He had no trouble selling his vegetables. Sometimes he gave food to people in return for a share of the gold they might find. One of the men he gave food to was John Gregory. In this way David Wall helped Gregory make his big discovery.

The Territory of Colorado

The gold rush brought a lot of people to the Pike's Peak region. Many of them did not find any gold and went back home. In 1861, two years after the first gold rush, more than 25,000 people were still living here.

These people did not have a government of their own. They could not make their own laws. The people in four different territories made the laws for them. The storekeepers in Denver lived in Kansas Territory. The people in Boulder lived in the Territory of Nebraska. Many of the miners lived in the Territory of Utah. The farmers in San Luis were part of the New Mexico Territory. This was very confusing to everyone. The people in the Pike's Peak region wanted to have a territory of their own.

The United States Congress passed a law in 1861 making a new territory for the Pike's Peak region. Before the law was passed, a question came up. What name should the new territory have? Many names were suggested.

Some were Indian names:

Tahosa — People who lived on the Mountain Top

Idaho — Gem of the Mountains

Yampa — Squaw Root

Arapaho — The Arapaho Indian Tribe

Others were Spanish names:

San Juan — Saint John

Colorado — Reddish color

Some were names of famous people:

Jefferson

Franklin

Columbus

Congress decided to give the new territory the name Colorado.

Which name do you like best?

The Colorado Territory was no longer just a gold mining region. Many people were coming to start new farms. Others began raising cattle to sell to the miners. They found that cattle liked the grass on the plains. The miners were glad to have fresh beef to eat. More and more settlers were moving to the new territory. They were coming to stay.

The Utes attacked this army train.

The Northern Utes were forced out of Colorado.

8

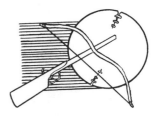

The Indians Leave Colorado

More and more people were coming to the territory of Colorado. They came across the plains by covered wagons and by stagecoaches. Along the river valleys, they plowed up more land for new farms. They put larger herds of cattle out to graze on the plains. On the land where Arapaho and Cheyenne tepees stood before, they built ranch houses and farm houses. New mining camps were built where the Utes once made their summer camps in the mountains. These new settlers were taking over the land which the Indians thought was theirs to use forever. What were the Indians to do?

The Plains Indians

At first, the Plains Indians tried to get along with these new people. They knew that if they attacked the wagons, soldiers in blue coats would come to fight with them. In years past, the Cheyennes had fought with the soldiers. Many of the Cheyennes were killed. The soldiers had more guns than they had. Besides, had not the Great Father, the President of the United States, promised that the plains would be their hunting ground forever? When the houses and stores were being built in Denver, the Arapahoes and Cheyennes even came in to watch. Sometimes the warriors left their wives and children camped near Denver when they went off to fight with the Utes. Some of the Indians and settlers became good friends.

Left Hand, an Arapaho chief, had many new settlers as friends. One was a rancher. Once, when Left Hand and his people camped nearby, the rancher came out with some food and presents. Left Hand liked this man and often came to visit him. Sometimes he would bring his wife and children. Many years later, the rancher's little girl remembered playing with the Indian children. She said, "We played with them and when they went they took some of our dresses and skirts with them. The next day they came back dressed in our clothes. One would have on an apron, another a skirt, and another a dress. They laughed and pointed to them, trying to tell us something in Indian."

Have you every played "dress up" like Left Hand's children did? Have you ever dressed up like an Indian?

It was not easy for the Indians and settlers to live in peace. They had different ideas on how to use the land. The Indians needed the open land as hunting grounds. The settlers wanted to own it, build fences across it, and dig ditches through it. The ranchers wanted the grass for their cattle. They thought that the Indians did not need all of the land. The Indians did not live by farming and raising cattle. They lived by hunting the buffalo, which needed wide, open spaces for grazing. The buffalo were afraid of places where many people lived, and so they began moving farther and farther away. It became harder for the Indians to find enough buffalo to eat. Soon they saw that the farms, ranches, and towns were crowding them off of their land.

The trouble began on the plains. When fewer and fewer buffalo were to be found, some of the Indians became angry. They raided the ranches and killed or

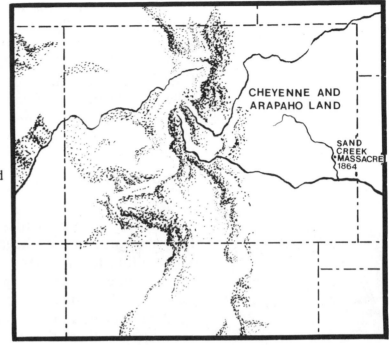

Cheyenne and Arapaho land

drove away the ranchers' cattle and horses. When they saw covered wagons and stagecoaches coming along the trails, the Indians attacked them. Some of the settlers were killed. This made the settlers angry and afraid. In the lonely ranch houses on the plains, families lived in fear of an Indian attack. The people in the towns heard stories about men being killed and women and children killed or taken away. They asked for the soldiers to come, but most of them were busy fighting a great Civil War in the East. Even though the Army had forts in the area, very few soldiers were there. The settlers decided that something would have to be done.

John Evans, who was then the Governor of Colorado Territory, ordered all of the Indians to move to the Army forts. If they would hand over their guns and bows and arrows, the soldiers would give them food. Those who would not move to the forts would be called "hostile" Indians. Then he ordered the settlers to kill any hostile Indians they might see.

Winter was coming and food was hard to find, and so many of the Plains Indians moved to the forts. Among them were Left Hand with the people from his Arapaho village and Black Kettle, chief of some of the Cheyennes. They camped near Fort Lyon at a place called Sand Creek. Putting up their tepees, they settled down for the winter. They did what John Evans had told them. They thought they would be safe.

Sand Creek

Many of the new settlers did not trust the Indians. They thought that the Cheyennes and Arapahoes were only waiting for a better chance to attack the settlements. Some thought the plains would not be a safe place until the Indians were punished. They wanted to fight the Indians and kill as many as they could. It did not matter to them that Black Kettle and many other Cheyennes and Arapahoes said they wanted to be friends with the new settlers. To them, all Indians would have to be punished and were to be feared.

One man who thought this way was John Chivington. Once a minister and later a soldier, Chivington was well liked by many people in Colorado. When he asked men to join the Army to fight the Indians, many people did so. For a while, Chivington and his soldiers guarded the stagecoaches on their way to Denver. Chivington wanted to fight a big battle to punish the Arapahoes and Cheyennes. With that in mind, he and his soldiers marched off toward Sand Creek. Left Hand, Black Kettle, and their people were not as safe as they had thought.

Early in the morning of November 29, 1864, Chivington and his men attacked the Indian camp at Sand Creek. The Indians were just waking up when the shooting began. When they ran out of their tepees to see what was happening, they were shot down. Women and children as well as men were killed that day. Black

Kettle could not believe it was happening. He stood by his tent with an American flag, hoping the men would see that they had made a mistake. The soldiers shot at him until he ran away. Left Hand also got away safely. White Antelope, a Cheyenne chief, would not leave. He stood beside Black Kettle's tepee with his arms folded, singing his death song:

> Nothing lives long.
> Nothing lives long.
> Nothing lives long.
> Except the earth and the mountains.

A few minutes later he was killed. No one knows how many Indians were killed that day. It was at least one hundred.

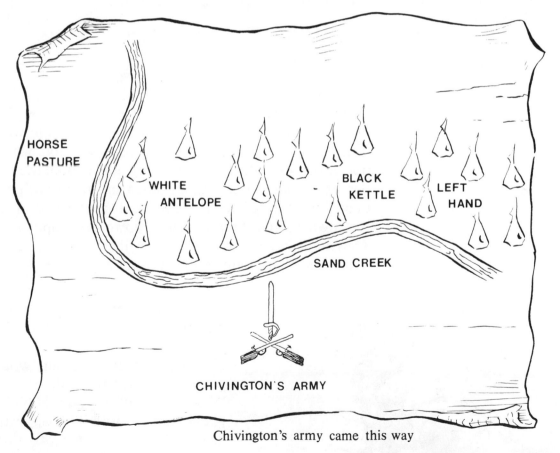

Chivington's army came this way

The attack at Sand Creek

After Sand Creek, most of the Arapahoes and Cheyennes saw that Colorado Territory was no longer a safe place to live. They moved to a reservation in what is now Oklahoma. Some of the younger warriors would not leave Colorado Territory. They attacked all the settlers they could find. Ranch houses and stagecoach stations were burned to the ground. They burned down the town of Julesburg and tore down telegraph lines. They, too, finally went to live on the reservation, but only after many fights with the soldiers.

If you had been a Plains Indian then, would you have continued to fight?
If you had been a settler, would you have fought the Indians?
What is an Indian reservation? If you do not know, look it up in the dictionary.

The last battle between Plains Indians and soldiers to take place in Colorado Territory was at Summit Springs. This is one page of a sketchbook that was found on the battle field. It was drawn by an Indian. Why do you think the horse in the center of the picture has no rider? Why do you think the guns of the soldiers were drawn to look as they do? What other things are happening in the picture? Who is winning this battle?

Life on the Reservation

Little Raven

Little Raven was one of the Arapaho chiefs. He tried to help his people learn to live on the reservation. When the government gave him a herd of cows, he worked hard to take care of them. When the government built him a house, he moved into it. Still, he was very lonesome for the old ways. He put his old tepee up in his front yard. Sometimes he would move out of his house to live in the tepee. After all, he was still an Arapaho.

Carl Sweezy was born on the reservation. He tells us how hard life was. "We had everything to learn about the white man's road," he said. This land was new to the Arapaho. Even the plants and animals were different. Learning to farm, to speak English, to wear close-fitting clothes, and even to cut their long braided hair was difficult. "We knew that our long braids and embroidered robes . . . and our tall, round lodges were much more beautiful," recalled Sweezy. Some of the things on the reservation surprised the Arapaho:

> "We thought windows were put in walls so that we might look in to see how the white people did their work and ate their meals and visited with each other.
> . . .
> "We pulled up some of the first little trees that were planted to see why white people had put sticks in the ground in rows."

Have you ever thought about why windows were in houses?
Have you ever wondered about how trees grow?
If you had been Little Raven, do you think you would rather have lived in a house or in a tepee?

If you had been Little Raven, do you think you would rather have lived in a house or in a tepee?

The Utes

The Utes were having problems, too. Settlers from the East wanted to move into the Ute lands to farm and raise cattle. The miners also caused a lot of trouble. They discovered gold in the Ute lands. They thought they had the right to mine the gold. After all, the Utes were not gold miners. They were hunters. The miners began to move into the Utes' land to mine the gold. The Utes had to decide what to do about this.

The Utes could let the miners and settlers have the land. They had given up land in the past. Once much of what is now Colorado was their hunting ground. Now only the western part of Colorado was left. If they gave that up, they would not have enough land for hunting. They would have to change their way of life. If they stopped hunting, they would have to settle down as farmers and ranchers.

The Ute chief, Ouray, thought the Utes should change their way of life. He knew that the soldiers would come to fight with them if they tried to drive the settlers and miners away. Then many Utes would be

From *Harper's Weekly,* October 25, 1879.

Chief Ouray

killed. Ouray decided to start a farm and to raise sheep. He left his tepee and lived in a house. The government of the United States built the house for him. Ouray told other Utes to start farms and ranches and not to attack the settlers.

Many of the Utes did not agree with Ouray. They wanted to live the way they had always lived. They did not want to change their way of life. Captain Jack and Douglas were two of the leaders of these Utes. They lived near the White River in western Colorado. The government had an Indian agency at the White River. It sent an agent to live there to show the Utes how to become farmers.

Captain Jack

The agent was Nathan Meeker. He wanted to help the Utes learn how to farm. For a while, the Utes listened to Meeker. They watched him and his men plow up some of the land to make farms. Some of them also sent their children to the school that Meeker started.

Nathan Meeker

Then one day Meeker did a foolish thing. He plowed up the Utes' race track to plant crops. The Utes liked to race their horses on the race track. They were very angry at Meeker. They did not want to become farmers if that meant not having a race track. So, Captain Jack, Douglas, and other Utes attacked Meeker and the other people at the agency. Meeker and all of the men who worked for him were killed. The women and children were taken away, but were set free after a few days.

Ouray had not been one of the Utes to fight at White River. He was asked by the soldiers to help make peace. There was no use fighting the soldiers anymore, he told the White River Utes. Ouray would not let the people of Colorado punish the Utes who had fought. Only Douglas was put in prison, and he was held only for a short time. The rest of these Utes were moved out of the area to a reservation in Utah.

The trip took two weeks. There were about 1,400 of these northern Utes. They had 10,000 sheep and goats and several thousand horses. By the time they reached the reservation in Utah, they had lost many of their animals. Some wandered away. Others were taken by ranchers who said they had been "stolen" by the Utes earlier. In the 1950s, the grandchildren of these Utes were paid money by the government for these lost animals.

Ouray went back to his own people, and he died not long after that. Most of the Utes were out of Colorado by then. A few southern Utes lived on a reservation in the southwestern part of the state. They still live there today.

Utes leaving Colorado

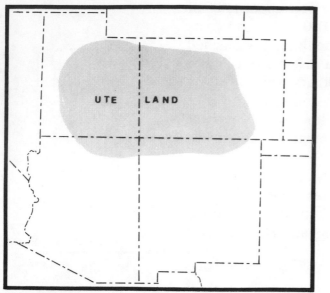

Early Ute land

Here is a map of the early Ute lands. Look at a map of the United States. What states did the Ute land cover?

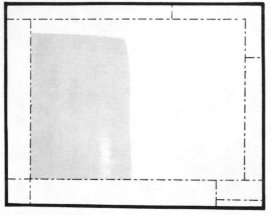

Ute land, 1868

Look at these maps of Colorado. How long did it take for the Utes to lose most of their land in Colorado? One time, when the government took more of the Ute lands, it said the rest would be kept by the Utes "as long as the rivers flow." Have you ever made a promise like that — one that you couldn't keep? Were the Americans wrong for thinking they could keep such a promise?

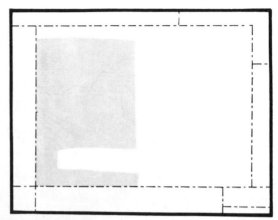

Ute land, 1873

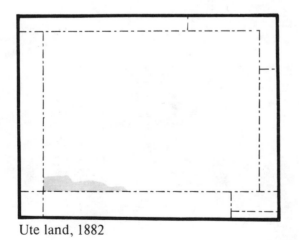

Ute land, 1882

Denver's first railroad depot

9

Living on the Land

Saturday, June 25, in the year 1870 was a very special day in Denver. The city park was decorated with flags, pine branches, and brightly colored pictures. Picnic tables were covered with pies and cakes. It was a special day because that morning the first railroad to Denver would be finished. A special train covered with flags had already arrived. A thousand people were waiting for John Evans to drive a silver spike into the last section of the iron rails. He picked up the hammer and drove in the spike. It was finished. Denver and Colorado Territory had a railroad.

Having a railroad was a great help to the new Colorado Territory. In the years to come, it would have many more. Railroads made it easier to bring people and things across the plains. Trains carried heavy loads to the mining camps in the mountains. They brought back gold and silver ore. Farmers and ranchers could use the railroads to send wheat, potatoes, and cattle to market. The railroads also helped to build new towns. The towns grew up around the railroad stations where cattle, food, and supplies were loaded and unloaded. Railroads helped the new Territory to grow.

In 1870 much of Colorado Territory was still unsettled. Very few people lived on the plains. The Arapaho and Cheyenne Indians had left to live on the reservations. Farmers and ranchers had settled along the Platte and Arkansas Rivers, but there was room for many more. The Spanish-Americans lived only in the southern part of the territory. The Utes had given up much of their old hunting ground. Supply towns and mining camps were the only large settlements. And they were scattered over the vast area of the Rocky Mountains. The new territory still had much empty space.

Has your family ever moved to a new home? Do you think the people in this picture enjoyed moving? Courtesy Solomon D. Butcher/Nebraska State Historical Society.

In the years after 1870, many new settlers came to Colorado. Most of them came from the states to the east and from New Mexico. They left their old homes to try to make a better living in Colorado. Many came from faraway countries. During these years, many thousands of people came to America from Germany, England, Ireland, and other countries. Many ended up in Colorado. Some even came from as far away as China. After 1900, some Japanese farmers also settled in Colorado. Most of the new settlers spoke English, but some did not. Many different languages were spoken in Colorado. Many different kinds of people came to live on the land.

Does anyone in your family speak any language other than English? Do you know any words in another language?

While many of the new settlers came by train, some still crossed the plains in covered wagons. It took more time, but it cost less money. Mary Jane Cole's family came out in two covered wagons in 1879. They tried to make the wagons as much like home as they could. Every two weeks they stopped for a day and did the family washing. They scrubbed and cleaned everything just as if they were at home. Even the chairs they brought along were taken out of the wagon and scrubbed. They even baked their own bread. Mary Jane told about the trip:

"During the day we mixed the bread in a large tin bucket, let it rise, and then would bake it when we camped for the night. As soon as a stopping place had been decided on, the stove was set off and the children scurried around for wood or buffalo chips. In the morning we made enough fire to get a light breakfast so the stove would not be too hot to load."

The River Valleys

Many people heard about the good farm land in Colorado. They knew that plants would grow if the fields could be watered. When they came, they looked for a place to live along the rivers and the creeks. Many settled along the Platte and the Arkansas Rivers, the two big rivers east of the mountains. It was easy to get land for a farm or cattle ranch. Most of the land was owned by the United States Government. The government would give people a farm if they would live on it for five years. This was called a homestead. Many of the early settlers were homesteaders. Others bought the land from someone who already owned it.

It took a lot of hard work to start a new farm. First, a house had to be built. A settler's first house was often a log cabin. The logs came from the cottonwood trees which grew along the banks of the streams. Then an irrigation ditch had to be dug, and the fields plowed and planted. The next job was to build a fence around the fields to keep cattle out. In the early days, cattle were put out to graze on the open plains. They liked the tender, young plants in a farmer's field. Only a strong fence could keep them out.

This man is beating the locusts away from his field with a branch from a tree. Some farmers went back East after locusts like these had eaten their crops. How would you have felt had you been this farmer? Courtesy Solomon D. Butcher/Nebraska State Historical Society.

Cattle were not the only animals who came to eat up the farmers' fields. Locusts were also a problem in the 1870s. The locust was like a grasshopper with wings. Big swarms of them came to the plains looking for food. In some years, there were so many of them that the sky was dark with flying grasshoppers. "They ate everything green," one early settler remembered. "We had planted some strawberries in the garden and put tin cans over them to shield them from the hot sun. The hoppers dug under these tins and ate the plants." When they were gone the farmers had to plant their fields over again. The locusts had eaten everything.

Some of the new settlers came out with just their families. Others came out in groups. They decided it would be easier if many people came out together. Then they could help each other build their houses and dig the ditches for water. If enough people came out, they could even build their own town. With a town they could have stores, shops, and maybe even a railroad station close by.

The best known of the group settlements in Colorado was Greeley. It was started in 1870 by a group led by Nathan Meeker. Meeker worked for an eastern newspaper. He had many ideas about how people could live and work together and wanted to try them out. The new Colorado Territory seemed like a good place to do it. He called a meeting to tell other people about his plans. The people who came to the meeting agreed that it was a good idea. Many of them wanted to come to Colorado with him. They decided to come out as a group and to name the new settlement Greeley. It was named after Horace Greeley, the editor of the newspaper for which Meeker worked.

They found a good place for the town of Greeley. The town was built close to the Platte River and next to the railroad to Denver. It was not a very pretty town, at

This was the new town of Greeley in 1870. Would you have been happy living in Greeley at that time?

first. There were a lot of tents, and the only buildings were log cabins and a hotel brought in from another town by the railroad. The land around the town was bare and flat. Some of the people who arrived in 1870 were very unhappy. Had they left their homes and friends to live in such an ugly little town? Some went back home, but others decided to work hard and to make Greeley a pretty town with shade trees and sidewalks. They dug ditches for water and planted the fields. Greeley soon became a big town with many good farms all around it.

In the years to come, group settlements were started in other places in Colorado. The town of Longmont was settled by people who came from the city of Chicago. Immigrant groups from Russia, Holland, and Sweden also started settlements. One little Swedish settlement in Colorado was called Ryssby. The families who lived there spoke the Swedish language. They also followed many of the customs they had learned at home.

Most of the settlers who came to Colorado were white people. But some black people also came to live here. Some were farmers, ranchers, and cowboys; others lived in towns and cities. The white people did not always treat the black people fairly. They did not let them have good jobs. They often made them live in their own part of town. The houses there were not very nice.

One black man, O. T. Jackson, wanted to make it easier for black people to become farmers. He started a settlement just for black people. More than sixty families joined him. They called their new settlement Dearfield. The settlers lived far away from the streams and creeks. They did not have much water for their fields. They had to work hard to grow anything. They said that they had to work so hard that the fields became very dear to them. That is why they named their settlement Dearfield.

Farmers also settled in the river valleys in western Colorado. This area was still the hunting ground of the Utes until 1881. In that year, the Utes were moved to reservations. Western Colorado was then opened to settlers.

People who had visited the Ute country knew that the land along the rivers was good farm land. As soon as the Utes left, farmers and ranchers rushed in. They settled first in the Colorado River valley. So many people came that a new town grew up almost overnight. This town, filled with tents and log cabins, was called Grand Junction. The land around it was soon taken up by farmers and ranchers. Other towns were built. The largest were Montrose and Delta.

Samuel Wade was a farmer who lived near the town of Delta. When he came there in 1881, he found some fruit trees and berry bushes growing wild. He thought it might be a good area for growing apples, pears, peaches, and other kinds of fruit. The next spring, he had young fruit trees brought in from the East. They arrived at the nearest railroad station during a snow storm. The snow was so deep that it took Wade nearly two weeks to get back to his farm. To keep the young trees from freezing, he built a fire every night beside the box they were in. He got them safely home and planted a big orchard. After that, other farmers also ordered fruit trees, and western Colorado became a famous fruit-growing area.

The Plains

The plains of eastern Colorado were still just big open spaces in 1870. People crossed the plains on wagon trails and a new railroad, but few people lived

Buffalo hides

there. The Indians had left, and most of the buffalo herds were gone. The rest of the buffalo were being killed by hunters from the East. They killed them by the thousands to make money by selling the buffalo robes.

Most of the land on the plains could not be irrigated. It was too far away from the rivers and streams. The short grass which grew on the plains was green in the spring. But it dried up and turned yellow in the summer heat. The early farmers thought that the plains were too dry for farming.

The early settlers did find one use for the plains. It was a good place for grazing cattle. People crossing the plains in wagons saw that their oxen and horses ate the yellow grass and liked it. The big herds of buffalo had liked it, too. These people also found out that cattle could live on the plains all year long.

Jack Henderson was one of the first settlers to discover that. Late in the year 1859, he brought wagons

Killing buffalo

filled with supplies out to the miners camped at Cherry Creek. It was too late in the winter for him to make the long trip back east. Having no hay to feed his oxen, he turned them loose on the plains. Then he forgot all about them. Surely they would starve to death on the plains. The next spring, Henderson went out on the plains to hunt buffalo. Much to his surprise, he found his oxen. They had not only lived through the winter, but they had grown fat eating the short, dried grass on the plains. After that, Henderson bought cattle and raised them on the plains.

The Plains Indians also knew a lot about the plains. Why did they not raise cattle on the plains?

Many of the new settlers in Colorado raised cattle. They started ranches and built ranch houses. Each ranch would also have a bunk house for the cowboys to sleep in and a corral for the horses. A big cattle ranch needed many cowboys and a lot of horses for them to ride. Most of the cattle in the early days came from the state of Texas. Big herds of a thousand or more cattle were driven north to Colorado. They were called Texas Longhorns. The cattle were let loose on the open plains to feed on the grass.

The cattle feeding on the plains belonged to many different ranches. In the early days, there were no fences on the plains, except those the farmers built. All the cattle grazed together. The ranchers branded the cattle so they could tell which animals belonged to them. A brand was a mark put on the side or hip of a cow or steer with a hot branding iron. Each owner had his own brand. Sometimes it was his initials. It might be any other mark which he decided would be his brand.

In the spring, the cowboys went out to round up the cattle. They had to find all the cattle that belonged to their ranch. After the young calves were branded, the

Each cattle ranch had many horses. Do you know why?

Texas longhorns

fatter cattle were sent off to market. They were driven to the nearest railroad and loaded onto the railroad cars. Sometimes the roundup took all summer. The cowboys spent several months living out on the plains. They slept in the open and ate at the chuck wagon. Each ranch had a chuck wagon and a cook. The chuck wagon followed the cowboys wherever they went until the roundup was over.

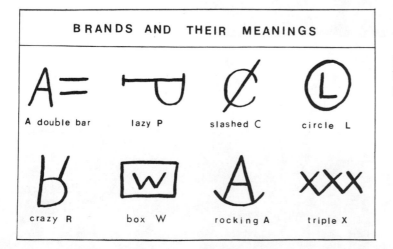

BRANDS AND THEIR MEANINGS

A double bar   lazy P   slashed C   circle L

crazy R   box W   rocking A   triple X

Every rancher had his own brand. Can you make up a brand for yourself?

138

Why was the chuck wagon so important to the cowboys? What things did the chuck wagon carry?

In the 1880s, some people moved out on the plains to try to farm. They saw that during some years it rained more than others. In the rainy years the grass stayed green late into the summer. They decided that they could raise corn, wheat, beans, and other things. By this time, most of the good farm land along the streams was already taken, and so hundreds of families moved to the plains to farm.

The settlers on the plains found a new way to build houses. They could not build houses of wood because there were no trees for miles around. Their houses were built out of sod. First they would plow up a strip of grass and dirt about three inches thick. Then they cut the strip into long flat pieces. These would be piled on

This is a sod house on the Colorado plains. How is it different from an adobe house? Why is grass growing on the roof?

top of each other to make the walls of the sod house. Sometimes the roof was also made of sod.

Etta Shannon grew up in a sod house on the plains north of Sterling. It was five miles to the nearest school. She and her sisters had to walk to school. It was easy to get lost walking across the plains. There were no trees and few fences or roads to help one find the way. Etta's father had to plow a furrow so the children could follow it to school. It was also very easy to get lost at night on the plains. There was one night that Etta would never forget.

One afternoon there was a big storm on the plains where Etta lived. As her father was away, her mother had to bring in the cows and calves. It rained so hard that she could not go out to look for them until it was almost dark. When the storm was over, her mother took Etta and her sisters out with her to look for the cattle. Night came before they had found them. In the dark, they took a wrong turn and got lost.

They spent the whole night lost on the plains. It was a very bad night. It rained and they were dripping wet. They were worried about the cattle and afraid of wild animals. When they heard some animal moving in the dark, they barked like dogs to scare it away. They did not find out where they were until daybreak came. They were four miles away from home. When they got back home, they found the cows and calves — they were safe at home, eating the grass nearby.

Have you ever been lost?
Can you imagine how Etta felt?

Farming on the plains was not an easy life. Many of the sod-house farms were miles away from the nearest town. In the winter, the cold winds blew the snow in drifts as high as the houses. Sometimes the snow blew so hard that one could not see three feet ahead. People got lost going from the house to the barn

This is how Colorado farmers harvested wheat and corn many years ago. What do farmers use today instead of horses and oxen?

to feed the cattle and horses. Some years, it would not rain very much. Then the corn and wheat would not grow. The farmers who had worked hard planting in the spring would have nothing to eat or to sell. In the dry summers, the farmers also had to worry about grass fires. Sometimes lightning would set the plains grass on fire. The fire would burn for miles and miles. Many farmers gave up and moved to some other place to farm.

Colorado Becomes a State

In 1876, there was another special day in Colorado. A big parade took place in Denver. Floats made of wagons covered with flags and banners moved down the main street. On the floats, girls in pretty dresses waved to the crowds of people along the way. Bands were playing, and people were cheering. After the parade, everyone walked down to a shady grove of trees beside the Platte River for a picnic.

This time, the people were not celebrating a new railroad. It was the Fourth of July, the birthday of the United States. This Fourth of July was a special birthday. The United States was one hundred years old. The people of Colorado had a very special reason to celebrate. It was their birthday, too. The people had just voted to become the nation's newest state, the State of Colorado.

For 15 years, Colorado had been only a territory of the United States. It was not equal to all the other states. People living in territories could not do some of the things that people living in states could do. They could not elect the man who would be their governor. They could not vote for the President of the United States. The people of Colorado thought it would be much better to become a state.

The Fourth of July is still an important day. How do people celebrate it now?

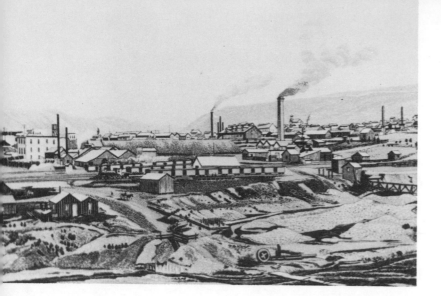

Many kinds of towns were built in Colorado.

10

Living in Towns and Cities

As time passed, more and more people in Colorado lived in towns and cities. Some people settled there when they first came to Colorado. Others moved to town from farms and ranches. People wanted to live in towns and cities for many reasons. Some thought they could make a better living there. They knew that their children would be closer to schools if they lived in a town, also. Other people were lonesome living out in the country. In town, they could live closer to friends and neighbors.

Colorado had many kinds of towns and cities. It had small towns, middle-sized towns, and big cities. There were mining towns, lumber towns, supply towns, and towns where people brought their crops and cattle to market. In the bigger cities, people did many different kinds of things. There were stores of all kinds, shops where saddles and wagons were made, and factories. The factories made tools, clocks, clothes, and many other things. The city of Pueblo even had a steel mill. The steel mill made rails for the railroads, wire for fences, and steel for making tools and machines.

All of the towns and cities had one thing in common. The people who lived there made a living in some way other than farming and ranching. Most of them did not work at home, either. They worked in shops and stores, offices, and factories. They left their homes in the morning and came back in the evening. They bought most of the food they needed. For people who had lived on farms, this was a new way of life.

Small Towns

Helen Howard was a young girl when her family moved to town. The Howards had lived on a ranch in Rio Blanco County before that. Very few people lived in that part of western Colorado. There were no schools for Helen to go to and no churches were nearby. Her father thought it would be better to live in a town. They decided to move to the little town of Rifle.

When they were ready to leave, the Howards loaded their furniture and other things into wagons. It took them two and one-half days to travel the 60 miles to Rifle. At night, the family slept beside the road in tents. "It was the first time my brother and I had camped out, and we thought it was great fun," Helen remembered. One night, they camped beside some apple trees. It was the first time Helen had ever seen fruit growing on trees. She picked a big, juicy apple and ate it. It tasted so good that she wanted more. "But my parents thought one was enough for a seven year old girl before going to bed."

Have you ever camped out?
Do you agree with Helen that camping out is fun?

The town of Rifle was not very big. When Helen's family moved there in 1902, about 300 people lived in Rifle. Helen's father bought a little three-room house with a shed for a kitchen. It did not even have grass for a lawn. The concrete sidewalk which Mr. Howard put in was the first one in town, but all the houses did have board fences around them. The fences kept out the cattle and horses that wandered around the town. Rifle was a market town for the ranchers nearby. Sometimes the cattle were driven through the middle of town on their way to the railroad. The children were told to run to the nearest house and to stay there until the cattle had passed.

The little town did not have many of the things bigger cities had. In many of the towns, there were no water pipes to bring water to the houses. Helen remembered how they got fresh water each day. "We bought water from a water wagon and stored it in barrels at the corner of the house. Howard Bartlett had one water wagon. Those who took water from him put out a blue flag." The other water man, Mr. Shipman, stopped at houses that put a red flag out as a signal for him. Helen's mother also bought fresh fruit and vegetables from a wagon that came by. This wagon driver would sing songs as he drove down the streets. The women always knew when the fruit wagon was coming.

W.M. Shipman delivered water to the houses in Rifle. This is W.M. Shipman. Can you tell what he is doing? Courtesy Rifle Reading Club, Rifle, Colorado.

Water coupon. Courtesy Rifle Reading Club, Rifle, Colorado.

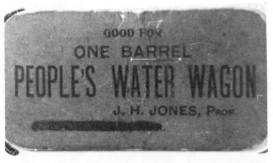

GOOD FOR
ONE BARREL
PEOPLE'S WATER WAGON
J. H. JONES, Prop.

When some of the little towns in Colorado began, there were not even any wood or brick buildings in the town. The first store in the town of Eagle was a tent. Charles F. Nogal, the owner, sold groceries, tools, seeds, cloth, milking pails, and kerosene for lamps. He put up a second tent as a saloon, where people could drink whiskey and play cards. The town did not yet have a hotel where travelers could stay over night, and so Mr. Nogal set up a third tent with beds in it. There was no place for people to eat. In a fourth tent, Mr. Nogal started a restaurant. Travelers and settlers could get a dinner of venison, potatoes, biscuits, fruit, and coffee for 25¢. Mrs. Nogal did the cooking. Later on, Mr. Nogal and other men put up log cabins and wood and brick buildings.

Charles Nogal standing beside his log cabin. Which would be better to live in, a log cabin or a sod house?

Most of the towns did have a livery stable. This was a place where horses were fed and kept overnight. A visitor could also rent a horse and buggy at the livery stable. Many of the horses owned by the livery stable were trained as "return" horses. Someone could rent a horse, ride to another town, and then tell the horse to go home. The horse would return to the livery stable all by itself.

Towns often had dressmaking shops. These were kept by women. Lena Propst opened a dressmaking shop in the town of Sterling. In those days, women did

Horses and buggy beside a livery stable in Rifle. Livery stable owners were very proud of their horses. Would you have been proud if these were your horses?

not go to a store to buy a dress. They had to make their own dresses or the dresses had to be made for them. Sometimes, Lena would go to their homes to make a dress; sometimes, the women went to her shop. She made the dresses by hand.

Before there were dress shops in Sterling, women would order cloth when the men went to Greeley for supplies. Once several men went together. They all bought the same color of cloth. That year most of the women and girls had black and red striped dresses just alike. They were glad to see a dress shop in Sterling. Then they could each choose the color they liked best.

New towns were also being built in southern Colorado. Many of them were coal-mining town. Coal was needed to make the railroad engines run, to burn in stoves in houses and to use in the factories. The steel mill at Pueblo needed a lot of coal for the big furnaces which melted iron ore into steel. Coal was found under the surface of the ground in many places in Colorado. Some of the best coal was found near Walsenburg and Trinidad in southern Colorado.

Coal mining would change the lives of many people in southern Colorado. It would change the lives of the Spanish-Americans most of all. They were among the first people to settle around Trinidad and Walsenburg. They lived as farmers and sheep herders. They spoke Spanish and followed many of the customs they brought with them from New Mexico. Many of the Spanish-Americans went to work in the coal mines. As coal miners, they could earn more money than they could as farmers. They lived in the coal-mining town with many other people. Their life was different after that.

Coal mining brought many new settlers to southern Colorado. These people came to work in the mines and in the stores and shops. Many of them did not like the Spanish-Americans. They did not like people whose customs were different from theirs. These new settlers did not always treat the Spanish-Americans fairly.

Tercio, Colorado
Tell what life would be like in
a town such as this.

Company Towns

Many of the coal-mining town were company
towns. They were built by the company which owned
the coal mines. These towns were not like Rifle or
Eagle, where anybody could live and own a house.
Only the people who worked for the company could
live in a company town. Single men lived in boarding
houses run by the company. The company owned the
houses in which men with families lived. The houses
were small and were not built very well. The companies knew that the coal would someday be mined
out. Then they would close up the mines and tear down
the houses. They did not want to spend money building
nice houses. Even the stores in the town were owned by

151

the company. The stores often charged high prices, but the miners had no place else to shop.

Were company towns nice places to live?
Why did people live in company towns?

A large number of the coal miners were immigrants. They had just come to the United States. They needed jobs and would work wherever they could. It was hard work digging coal out of the mines. It was

Louis Tikas

dangerous, too. Sometimes the coal dust would explode. Sometimes the coal caught on fire. Many miners were hurt or killed when they were using the machines that dug out the coal. Many of them could not speak English. Sometimes five or six languages were spoken in a town. It was not easy for the immigrants to find better jobs.

Louis Tikas was an immigrant from Greece who worked in a coal mine in southern Colorado. He wanted the company to make it safer to work in coal mines. He also wanted better wages for the miners and better houses for them to live in. The company did not want to do these things. It would cost them more money. Louis Tikas got many of the miners together in protest. Men with guns were brought in by the company. The Governor of Colorado sent in soldiers. They fought a battle with the miners, and many people were killed. One of the men who was killed was Louis Tikas. Later on, the miners did get better wages, and the mines were made safer.

Lumber companies also built company towns. These were companies that cut down trees in the forests and sawed the logs into boards. McPhee, Colorado, was a lumber company town that was built near the town of Dolores. Chopping down trees and sawing logs was also dangerous work. The men often got hurt. Because of this, the town of McPhee soon had a doctor's office as well as a store, a school, and houses for the workers. It was even a dangerous place for the doctor.

The doctor at McPhee was Dr. Speck. He spent a lot of his time taking care of workers in the logging camps out in the forest. To get there, he rode a little railroad car which had a motor. The trains were supposed to wait until Dr. Speck was off the track. Once a train engineer was not told that Dr. Speck was coming. The doctor saw the train coming just as he rounded a curve. He jumped off his car just in time.

Some of the workers at McPhee lived better than others. The Spanish-American and Mexican workers were treated the worst. They had their own area of town to live in. It was not as nice as other parts of town. The houses were smaller. The wages they received were not as good as the wages that other workers received. Still, many Spanish-American and Mexican workers came to work at McPhee. Jobs were hard to find. To

153

take care of their families, they had to work wherever they could.

McPhee, Colorado

Opposite below, and *right,* these are lumbermen near McPhee. Can you tell what kinds of work they are doing?

Mining Towns

Many of the people who came to Colorado lived in the mining towns up in the mountains. After John Gregory's discovery in 1859, gold was found in many other places. The miners also found silver in the mountains of Colorado. Often the mines went deep into the mountainsides. Sometimes, whole sides of mountains were dotted with mine shafts. When very much gold or silver was found, a new mining town was started.

The mining towns that were started in places rich with gold or silver grew very rapidly. People swarmed in to work in the mines and to open stores and shops in town. Others worked in the stamp mills. The stamp mills were big buildings with heavy machines that crushed the rock which held the gold or silver. Later the gold or silver was melted into bars. Other men cut down trees for timber to be used in the mines. The logs and boards were used to keep the mine shaft from caving in. There was much work to be done in a mining town.

Many of the mining towns in Colorado were known throughout the world. Leadville was a famous silver mining town. It was so high up in the mountains that it was nicknamed "Cloud City." Cripple Creek was

155

Leadville

a gold mining town. It was near Pike's Peak. Other mining towns were started in the San Juan Mountains in southwestern Colorado. Silverton and Ouray were two of the San Juan mining towns. Many people came to these towns from the eastern states and from other countries.

Can you think of how Silverton and Leadville got their names?
Can you think of how Ouray got its name?

Loading bars of silver

When Mabel Barbee was a young girl, her father went to Cripple Creek to look for gold. Later he sent for Mabel and her mother. As the railroad had not yet reached Cripple Creek, they had to go by stagecoach. It was a very exciting trip for Mabel.

One night, the stagecoach was stopped as it was going up a mountain road. Two men with masks on their faces stepped out of the dark. They made the people get out and line up beside the stagecoach. They were robbers. The robbers wanted their money, rings, and watches. In her pocket, Mabel had a silver dollar which her mother had given her. She tried to think of a way to hide it so the robbers would not find it. She thought of putting it in her stocking, but she could not do that because the robbers would see her doing it. Then she had an idea. While she pretended to scratch her nose, she slipped the silver dollar into her mouth. It was such a big coin she could hardly breathe. But maybe it would be safe.

Mabel was standing at the end of the line. When one of the robbers got to her, he held his lantern up to her face. Then he started laughing. The silver dollar was so big that Mabel had not been able to close her mouth. Anybody could have seen it. The robber thought it was funny. He took a silver dollar out of his pocket and put it on top of Mabel's. Then the robbers left with everybody's money but Mabel's. She had twice as much money as before.

Her father met them at the stagecoach station and took them home. Home in the new mining town was a tent. It had a stove, chairs, a homemade table, and a lumpy mattress on an old wooden bed. Later they lived in a wooden house and even had a piano. Many people lived in tents when a mining town was getting started. That night, even a tent looked good. It was much better than a stagecoach being held up by robbers.

Why did people in new mining towns live in tents?
Would a tent be good to live in during the winter?

The Big Cities

Some of the towns of Colorado were growing into cities. More and more people came to live in them. The largest city of all, Denver, had more than 133,000 people by the year 1900. Pueblo and Colorado Springs were smaller, but they were growing into big cities, too. The railroads made it easy for people to come from miles around to buy and sell things in these cities. Farmers and ranchers brought their crops and cattle in to market. The cities had hotels, department stores, and many kinds of shops. They also had factories where wagons, tools, and other things were made. There were many kinds of jobs for people to work at in the cities. Many people worked in the steel mill at Pueblo and in the smelters at Denver and Colorado Springs.

The cities had many things that small towns did not have. They had water piped into the houses. In small towns, people got their water from a pump or from a water wagon. Before there were electric lights, the cities had gas lights for homes. Gas lights also lit the streets at night. People in the small towns and in the country still used kerosene lamps. The cities had hospitals, libraries, and big parks. Denver and Colorado Springs had zoos. They also had streetcars to help people get around.

Do cities still have things that small towns do not have?

When towns were small, people could walk wherever they wanted to go. As the towns grew into cities, it was harder to get around. Often it was too far to walk from home to downtown or to school or work. There were no automobiles or buses in those days. Many city people did not own a horse. The cities had to find a way to make it easy for people to go where they wanted.

To make it easier to get around in Denver, some people started a street railway. The railway had a car which ran on two rails in the middle of the street. One or two horses would pull the car along. As many as 20 people could ride at one time. It was faster than walking, but the horse-cars were still very slow. After a while, electric streetcars or trolleys were invented. The trolleys still ran on rails, but an electric motor made them move. They were much faster than horse-cars.

In time, trolley-car lines were built farther and farther from the center of Denver. People could build their houses out on the edge of the city and ride the trolley to work. Then people could live almost in the country and work and shop in the city. Many new suburbs were built on the trolley lines.

People could also use the trolleys to go out of the city to the new parks around Denver. They could have

Can you figure out how this electric trolley worked?

This horse car went up a steep hill. The horse had to work hard to get the car to the top, but he probably enjoyed the ride back down.

picnics, swim, play baseball, or go rock climbing. Some of the parks were owned by the city. Some were amusement parks where people had to pay. One amusement park was Elitch Gardens. It had a small zoo and rides for the children. The adults could go to the dance hall or the theater. Bands played in the park, and there was even a restaurant.

Mary Elitch in bear pit

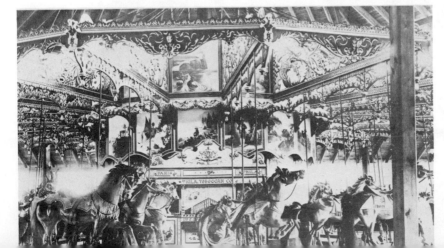

Fun at Elitch Gardens

In those days, many people used bicycles to get around. For a while, it seemed that everyone in Colorado rode a bicycle — even doctors, teachers, and housewives. Some people belonged to bicycle clubs. They would take trips on Sundays and holidays just for the fun of it. There were many parks and lakes for families to go on bicycles for a picnic.

Towns and Cities Today

Today most of the people in Colorado live in towns and cities. Some are small towns, and a few are still mining towns. The towns and cities are different from those of the past. City buses have replaced the trolleys. Electric lights have taken the place of gas lights. Almost everyone gets water from a faucet. There are still many bicycles, but most people use automobiles for getting around. Most streets are so crowded with automobiles that they are not safe for riding bicycles. Yet in many ways, living in towns and cities today is not so different from the past. People who live in towns and cities have neighbors close by. They work in stores, shops, offices, and factories. Even though they may have a garden, they buy most of the food that they need. They are close to libraries, hospitals, parks, and can visit zoos. They still live a town and city way of life.

People enjoy many ways of life in Colorado.
Photographs by Jeff Metcalf.

11

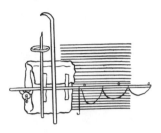

The Land and the People of Today

Many, many changes have taken place since the first unknown men came to this land we call Colorado. How surprised they would be to see how many people live here today. How puzzled they would be as they watched people using the land in so many different ways. They would wonder about all the many machines and tools, but some things would seem the same to them. They would still see the plains, the mountains, the plateaus, and the rivers. They would still see some of the plants and animals that they knew.

The Plains

The plains make up two-fifths of Colorado. They are huge, grass-covered, treeless stretches of land. They are still dry and harsh lands on which to live. The people who live there now are very different from the first people on the land. They use the land in very different ways.

If you live on the plains or go to visit them, you can see many of the things that early man knew. You can look for cottonwood and willow trees along the rivers. You can find yucca, cactus, and buffalo grass. You might see antelope, coyotes, jack rabbits, prairie dogs, or pheasants. These things have lived on the plains for thousands of years.

Where the plains meet the mountains, there is a strip of land about 30 miles wide. It stretches from Wyoming to New Mexico. It is in this area that two-thirds of Colorado's people live.

Yucca

Jack rabbit

Buffalo grass

The Mountains

Another two-fifths of the land of Colorado is covered by mountain ranges. They are all part of a great chain of mountains that sweep from the Arctic Circle to northern New Mexico. In this whole long chain, there are only fifty-four peaks higher than 14,000 feet. All of them are in Colorado. There are a thousand other peaks which reach 10,000 feet.

The mountains have been the most important feature in Colorado. They catch the snow which melts into the rivers that irrigate the farms of our state and eighteen other states. The mountain streams are the homes of the beaver which brought the fur trappers to the land. Mountains held the gold and the silver which brought the miners to seek their fortunes. Now they are used for other things as well.

You have to have sharp eyes to see many of the animals of the mountains. Bears, squirrels, weasels, elk, deer, and mountain lions can be found up to about 10,000 feet. They hide among the spruce, pine, balsam, and fir trees. Higher up, above 11,500 feet, no trees can grow. There is little soil, and it never gets very warm. Here you will find a few hardy mountain sheep, the tiny pika, and the ptarmigan bird. They feed on lichen, mosses, alpine flowers, and a few other small plants.

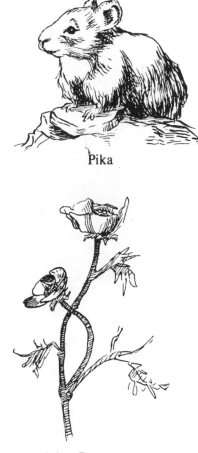

Pika

Alpine Buttercup

Deer

Plateaus

The western one-fifth of Colorado is part of a huge area of land known as the Colorado Plateau. Do you remember what mesa means? There are many mesas, deep valleys, and canyons on this land. Many of the streams and rivers on this side of the Continental Divide meet here to form the mighty Colorado River.

People who live on the Colorado Plateau also use the land in many different ways.

There are many kinds of plants and animals on the plateau. In some places, there are yellow pine, Douglas fir, and mountain maple. Other places have aspen and spruce trees. Sage brush can be found here, as well as in eastern Colorado. The animals are the same as are found in the lower mountains — deer, rabbits, mountain lions, and coyotes.

Rocky Mountain maple

Mountain lion

Coyote

Our State Emblems

Every state has special signs and emblems. These are usually things that are important to the people. Here are the meanings for Colorado's emblems.

The State Seal
This was made before Colorado was a state. It shows the eye of God, and the Latin words mean "Nothing Without Providence." What was added after Colorado became a state? What are the tools shown on the shield?

The State Flag
The blue is for the Colorado skies. Red is for the color of the soil, and the gold is for the metal. The white represents the mountain snows.

The State Flower
The Rocky Mountain columbine was chosen as the state flower. It also has blue for the skies, white for the snow, and gold for the metal. It is against the law for anyone to pick the wild columbine. There are not very many of them left.

The State Bird

The lark bunting is our state bird. It sings while it is flying. Deep blue or dark gray in color, it can be seen all over the state.

The State Tree

The Colorado blue spruce is the state tree. Although it grows wild in only part of the state, it can be planted anywhere. Sometimes it is almost blue in color. Sometimes it is almost silver.

The State Animal

Not every state has a special animal. Colorado adopted the Rocky Mountain bighorn sheep because this is one of the few places where it is found. It is a very brave and strong animal that lives high on the mountain slopes.

The People

Many different kinds of people live in Colorado today. Some were born here; others have moved to the state. Most of them think this is a good place to live.

Photo by Jeff Metcalf.

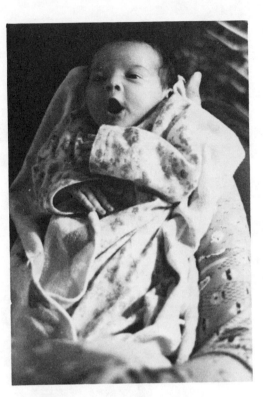

Photo by Jeff Metcalf.

Some of Colorado's people live on farms.
Photo by Jeff Metcalf.

Many more of them live in towns or large cities. Photo by Stewarts, courtesy Colorado Springs Chamber of Commerce.

The Utes still have a tiny bit of their old homeland in the southwestern part of the state.

Other Native Americans live in the cities of Denver and Boulder.

These Sioux girls are ready for a pow wow. Photos by Jeff Metcalf.

Some Spanish-Americans still live on the land their families settled such a long time ago. Some Colorado people have come from Mexico. They live in many places in the state. In some of their schools they learn their lessons in both Spanish and English. Photos by Jeff Metcalf.

174

Children of many other ethnic groups live
in Colorado. Photos by Jeff Metcalf.

Courtesy Boulder Chamber of Commerce.

For people who live in Colorado there are many exciting things to do.

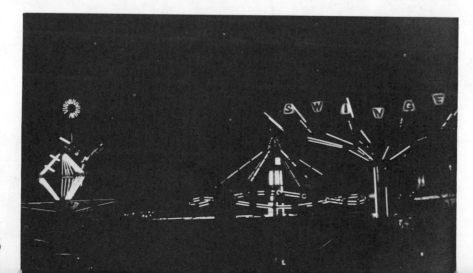

Sometimes the children of Colorado watch others perform. Courtesy Colorado Springs Chamber of Commerce.

Sometimes they make their own fun. Photo by Jeff Metcalf.

Sources

The authors used many books, articles, and collections of unpublished materials in writing this book. We have included in this brief and selected bibliography the most important of those sources. These sources will also be useful for teachers who want additional information. Books for students are listed in the accompanying *Activities Booklet and Teachers' Guide.*

The two general histories of Colorado which we found most useful are LeRoy R. Hafen, ed., *Colorado and Its People* (4 vols., New York, 1948) and Carl Ubbelohde, Maxine Benson, and Duane A. Smith, *A Colorado History* (3rd. ed., Boulder, 1972).

Many good books exist for the native American inhabitants of Colorado. The story of prehistoric man from early times through the Cliff Dwellers can be found in C.T. Hurst, *Colorado's Old Timers: The Indians Back to 25,000 Years Ago* (Gunnison, Colo., 1946) and Don Watson, *Indians of the Mesa Verde* (Mesa Verde National Park, 1961). Our chapter on Mesa Verde is heavily indebted to Watson's book. The best account of the evolution of Ute culture is Marvin K. Opler, *The Southern Ute of Colorado,* reprinted from *Acculturation in Seven American Indian Tribes* (New York, 1940). Many interesting aspects of Ute culture are examined topically in James Jefferson, Robert W. Delaney, and Gregory C. Thompson, *The Southern Utes: A Tribal History* (Ignacio, Colorado, 1972). The two standard books on the Plains Indians in Colorado are Virginia Cole Trenholm, *The Arapahoes, Our People* (Norman, 1970) and George Bird Grinnell, *The Cheyenne Indians: Their History and Ways of Life* (2 vols., New York, 1962). E. Adamson Hoebel, *The Cheyennes: Indians of the Great Plains* (New York, 1960) also contains much that is interesting on Cheyenne culture.

The history of Indian-settler conflict is detailed in several books. The most useful for the episodes which we recounted are Stan Hoig, *The Sand Creek Massacre* (Norman, 1961) and Marshall Sprague, *Massacre: The Tragedy at White River* (Boston, 1957). The impact of reservation life on the Indians is graphically portrayed in Althea Bass, *The Arapaho Way: A Memoir of an Indian Boyhood, by Carl Sweezy* (New York, 1966).

We found several valuable sources for Spanish-American history and culture. Francis T. Cheetham, "The Early Settlements of Southern Colorado," *Colorado Magazine,* V (February 1928) pp. 1-8 and Luis Baca, "The Guadalupita Colony of Trinidad," *ibid.,* XXI (January 1944), pp. 22-27, provide general background on the settlements. Aspects of the early Spanish-American way of life are described in Olibama Lopez, "Pioneer Life in the San Luis Valley," *ibid.,* XIX (September 1942), pp. 161-167, Orlando L. Sandoval, "Recreational Activities of the Early Spanish Settlers in the San Luis Valley," Masters Thesis, Adams State College, Alamosa, Colorado, 1959, and in the Charles Hayden Papers in the Western History Collection, University of Colorado Library.

Various phases of Anglo-American settlement are dealt with in the first two volumes of Hafen, ed., *Colorado and Its people,* and in Ubbelohde, Benson, and Smith, *A Colorado History.* The literature on this period of Colorado history is quite extensive. A great deal of general information can be found in David Lavender, *Bent's Fort* (New York, 1954), Duane Smith, *Rocky Mountain Mining Camps: The Urban Frontier (Bloomington, 1967), Ora Brooks Peake, The Colorado Range Cattle Industry (Glendale, 1937), and Alvin T. Steinel, History of Agriculture in Colorado* (Fort Collins, 1926).

By far the richest sources for Anglo-American social and cultural history are personal memoirs and local histories. Anne Ellis, *The Life of an Ordinary Woman* (Boston, 1929) and Mabel Barbee Lee, *Cripple Creek Days* (Garden City, New York, 1958) are fascinating accounts of life in mining camps. Life in other types of communities is described in detail in MacDonald Knight and Leonard Hammock, *Early Days on the Eagle* (Eagle, Colorado, 1965), Rifle Reading Club, *Rifle Shots* (Rifle, Colorado, 1973), Sylvia McClellan, *Timber: The Story of McPhee, The Largest Lumbering Camp in Colorado* (Dolores, Colorado, 1970), and Ruth Schooley Hall, *Soddie Bride* (Fort Collins, 1973). We also found many interesting accounts of pioneering in Colorado in unpublished materials at the Colorado State Historical Society Library and in issues of the *Colorado Magazine.*

Local histories exist for many towns and cities of Colorado. Two useful guides for identifying them are Colorado Association of School Librarians, *Colorado Grubstake '76: A Comprehensive Collection of Currently Available Materials About Colorado* (Littleton, Colorado, 1975), pp. 58-66 and Virginia Lee Wilcox, *Colorado: A Selected Bibliography of Its Literature, 1858-1952* (Denver, 1954).

Valuable sources for the natural history of Colorado include John and Halka Chronic, *Prairie, Peak, and Plateau* (Denver, 1972), George W. Kelly, *A Guide to the Woody Plants of Colorado* (Boulder, 1970), and Tim W. Kelley, *Living in Colorado* (Boulder, 1969).